Presented to:

~~~~~~~~~~~~~~~~~~~~~~~~~~~~~~~~~~~~~~~~~~

From:

~~~~~~~~~~~~~~~~~~~~~~~~~~~~~~~~~~~~~~~~~~

Date:

~~~~~~~~~~~~~~~~~~~~~~~~~~~~~~~~~~~~~~~~~~

# · LIVE ·
# BRAVE

Devotions, Recipes, Experiments, and
Projects for Every Brave Girl

◆

WRITTEN BY TAMA FORTNER

ILLUSTRATIONS BY
OLGA AND ALEKSEY IVANOV

Tommy NELSON®

An Imprint of Thomas Nelson

*Live Brave: Devotions, Recipes, Experiments, and Projects for Every Brave Girl*

© 2020 Thomas Nelson

Tommy Nelson, PO Box 141000, Nashville, TN 37214

Published in Nashville, Tennessee, by Tommy Nelson. Tommy Nelson is an imprint of Thomas Nelson. Thomas Nelson is a registered trademark of HarperCollins Christian Publishing, Inc.

Written by Tama Fortner. The writer is represented by Cyle Young of C.Y.L.E. (Cyle Young Literary Elite, LLC), a literary agency.

Illustrations by Olga and Aleksey Ivanov.

Tommy Nelson titles may be purchased in bulk for educational, business, fund-raising, or sales promotional use. For information, please e-mail SpecialMarkets@ThomasNelson.com.

Scripture quotations marked **ICB** are taken from the International Children's Bible®. Copyright © 1986, 1988, 1999 by Thomas Nelson. Used by permission. All rights reserved.

Scripture quotations marked **THE MESSAGE** are from *The Message*. Copyright © by Eugene H. Peterson 1993, 1994, 1995, 1996, 2000, 2001, 2002. Used by permission of NavPress. All rights reserved. Represented by Tyndale House Publishers a Division of Tyndale House Ministries

Scripture quotations marked **NCV** are from the New Century Version®. © 2005 by Thomas Nelson. Used by permission. All rights reserved.

Scripture quotations marked **NIV** are from the Holy Bible, New International Version®, NIV®. Copyright © 1973, 1978, 1984, 2011 by Biblica, Inc.® Used by permission of Zondervan. All rights reserved worldwide. www.Zondervan.com. The "NIV" and "New International Version" are trademarks registered in the United States Patent and Trademark Office by Biblica, Inc.®

Scripture quotations marked **NKJV** are from the New King James Version®. © 1982 by Thomas Nelson. Used by permission. All rights reserved.

Scripture quotations marked **NLT** are from the Holy Bible, New Living Translation. © 1996, 2004, 2007, 2013, 2015 by Tyndale House Foundation. Used by permission of Tyndale House Ministries, Carol Stream, Illinois 60188. All rights reserved.

### Library of Congress Cataloging-in-Publication Data

Names: Fortner, Tama, 1969- author. | Ivanov, O. (Olga), illustrator. | Ivanov, A. (Aleksey), illustrator.
Title: Live brave : devotions, recipes, experiments, and projects for every brave girl / written by Tama Fortner; iIllustrations by Olga and Aleksey Ivanov.
Description: Nashville, Tennessee : Thomas Nelson, [2020] | Series: Brave girls | Audience: Ages 8-12 | Audience: Grades 4-6 | Summary: "Live Brave is the latest devotional in the Brave Girls series for your tween, including 90 all-new devotions and 30 hands-on activities to encourage girls to get creative, have fun, and take their faith out into the world"—Provided by publisher.
Identifiers: LCCN 2019059079 | ISBN 9781400219599 (hardcover)
Subjects: LCSH: Girls--Prayers and devotions--Juvenile literature. | Girls--Religious life--Juvenile literature. | Religious education--Activity programs--Juvenile literature.
Classification: LCC BV4860 .F67 2020 | DDC 242/.62--dc23
LC record available at https://lccn.loc.gov/2019059079

*Printed in China*

20 21 22 23 24   DSC   10 9 8 7 6 5 4 3 2 1

**Mfr: DSC / Shenzhen, China / July 2020 / PO #9589590**

# Meet the Brave Girls

## Hope

Ready for a game of football? Yeah, I know I'm a girl. And girls aren't supposed to play football, right? Well, you haven't seen me with my brothers. Every Saturday afternoon we're out in the yard playing flag football with our neighbors. And if it isn't football, it's soccer or softball. We even have a volleyball net! I guess that's one advantage to living on a farm outside of town—plenty of room to play hard.

I actually have a girly side to me that likes to dress up and be pretty and all that stuff. But give me a pair of broken-in jeans, a T-shirt, and a good group of friends, and I'm happier than a homecoming queen.

I guess you could say nothing in my life is all that fancy. Farm life just isn't that way. But I have a terrific family. I'm the oldest, and my two younger brothers are twins my parents adopted from Ukraine when they were two years old. I love those guys, even though they bother me sometimes. We all work together around the farm and around our church. We help out with the local charity too because we can't get over how good God has been to us. And sharing His hope with others? Well, it beats football any day.

I do admit that I have a challenge I don't like to talk about: reading. I do okay in school for the most part. But when I read, the letters get mixed up, and sometimes it looks like another language to me. They call it dyslexia. I call it embarrassing. But I do my best to remember that God can help me tackle this challenge. And He's where I'm learning to put my—you guessed it—hope!

# Glory

If you could be anywhere in the world right now, where would you be? I'm kind of torn. Half of me would want to be on a high mountain somewhere, enjoying a beautiful sunset. Or maybe the beach, looking out across the sparkling waters. But the other half of me would be just as wonderstruck walking down the streets of New York City with my mom and sisters, shopping for all the latest fashions! I mean, you can never have enough boots, right? Or scarves and earrings and nail polish to match?

Yes, I know it might sound weird, but there is a common thread to everything I love: beauty! I love beauty wherever I see it: in this awesome world God created, in a gorgeous dress in a store window, and in the great hugs I get from my friends. I think God's beauty is everywhere—you just have to look for it.

Lately, I've had to look a little harder. Life at home wasn't so pretty, and just last summer my parents got divorced. For a while, I got really mad at God and forgot about the good in the world. But then my friends from the youth group started writing me encouraging notes and inviting me over. Their love and friendship was, well, beautiful—and it got me noticing all the other amazing ways God shows His love to me. I've started to see how God can take even the ugly, hard things in life and turn them into something good. I'm working on forgiving my parents and praying that God will use me to encourage other girls like me. You know, God can take even the messiest of situations and use it for His glory!

# Honor

My friends say that whenever and wherever there's a challenge, I'm the one to take it! Maybe that's why I always pick up stray animals and bring them home. I love to care for my furry friends and figure out how to make them better. I'm always going to the library to find new books to help me in my animal rescue mission! In fact, I love to read books in general. Last summer I started volunteering at the library so that I could help other kids learn to love books too.

But my biggest challenge lately hasn't been at the library or with my five pets. It's been at school. Studying has always been easy for me, and I was thrilled when the principal said I could skip a grade. But I had a really hard time fitting in with the older kids. They didn't seem impressed with my intelligence, so at first I tried dressing and talking more like they did, even though I knew it didn't honor God. That didn't work either.

I just ended up feeling guilty and more out of place than ever. Turns out they weren't the kind of friends I needed anyway. It's a good thing God has given me an awesome youth group. My leader and friends there have helped me remember who God says I am.

So who am I, really? You could say I'm God's girl, even though I don't *always* act like it. But I am learning how to honor Him more. And one day I hope to take all the abilities God has given me and use them, maybe to become a veterinarian or zoologist or something. Whatever I do, though, one thing's for sure: I want it all to honor God.

## Gracie

Let's just say it's all by God's grace that I'm here. And I'm not just saying that because of my name. If it had been left up to me, I'd still be in my old hometown of Perkasie, Pennsylvania. We're talking beautiful green hills and parks on every street corner. I was born there, and I knew everybody (and everybody knew me).

And then we moved. I thought life was over. I wanted my old friends and old world back, and I was pretty stubborn and loud about it.

In my hometown, my family and I didn't talk about God much. But once we moved here, we started going to this church, and there were some girls in the youth group who were . . . nice. More than nice, really. They were cool. They liked to do fun stuff and all, but they also weren't afraid to talk about things that matter—like what we're supposed to do with our lives. I used to ask myself that question sometimes, like when I was walking through the woods by my house or listening to my music. These girls were able to show me the answer in the Bible. I always knew there had to be a God who made all those beautiful things. Now I'm beginning to know who He is, thanks to God Himself, those girls, my church, and, yes, even my parents, who moved me here.

Wanna know something else kind of funny? The only time I ever sang back in Pennsylvania was in my shower at home. I loved it, but I was afraid to sing in public. Now I'm in the choir at church, and I'm singing about God to anybody who'll listen!

## Faith

Have you ever known anybody who is homeschooled? If you haven't, now you do! My sister and I have been homeschooled all our lives. I miss my friends, but I still love learning at home because I have more time—to finish my work, to hang out, and to think. I've even used that time to start reading the Bible on my own because I really want to make God happy.

But to tell you the truth, I tend to try to please more than just God. I want everyone to like what I do, which has made me quite a perfectionist. Even though my name is Faith, I think a better name right now would be Worry because I'm always worried that I'm going to disappoint someone, including myself. The only time I get away from those thoughts is when I'm painting, my favorite hobby. Fortunately, I find lots of time for that, which is starting to pay off. I've been asked to help the younger kids with their art projects at camp this year, and I've even won some local art contests!

The girls in the youth group are helping me too, and I love spending time with them. They remind me that God already knows all about my mess-ups and sins but loves me anyway. I guess I'm learning that my faith is not a bunch of "dos and don'ts." It's about a relationship with God, who knows the *real* me, and He is working on me to make me more like Him. That's what real faith is all about—believing that God loves me, forgives me, and sees me as His very own work of art, no matter what!

# The Youth Group

If God had thought we worked better alone, He wouldn't have invited so many people into His family. We need each other! Just like a body works best when all its parts are connected, God's family is the strongest when all His kids work and worship together.

But a funny thing often happens with a big group of people who spend a lot of time together. The people start to look the same. They dress the same, talk the same, and only welcome other people who are, well, just like them. Think about your body: Can you imagine if your nose decided to be an eye instead? And then, out of peer pressure, your ear became an eye, then your hands, and . . . you get the picture. You'd have a body of eyes without any ability to move, feel, taste, touch, or smell. Plus, you'd creep out a lot of people.

Each one of us has a special way to honor God and help others see Him in ways the rest of us can't on our own. But together, we're even stronger—which is a great part of God's plan.

That's what our youth group is all about: learning how to work together to know God better and to tell other people about Him too. We meet every week to talk, to learn what God is saying to us in the Bible, and to pray about anything and everything—together, the way God's family was meant to be. Want to join us?

# FULL OF FUN

"A thief comes to steal . . . but I came to give life—life in all its fullness."
—JOHN 10:10 NCV

A lot of people seem to think that following God isn't much fun. Some people will even say the Christian life is just a bunch of rules about what you can and can't do. That's so wrong!

When you decide to live a brave life for God, He'll take you on the most amazing, exciting adventure you'll ever have. Trust us, we know!

We're the Brave Girls. We call ourselves that because there are times when it really does take a lot of courage to do the right thing and follow God. But do you know what else we've learned? Following God can be a blast! That's what Jesus meant when He said that He came to give us "life in all its fullness." God wants to fill your life up to the top with His goodness and joy. Will there still be some tough times to work through? Yeah. But when we have faith in Him, God gives us the courage to do all kinds of brave—and fun—things for Him. Are you ready to live a life filled with love, hope, friendship, adventure, and *lots* of laughter? Are you ready to live brave?

## A BRAVE GIRL'S PRAYER

Holy Father, please show me how living for You really can be joyful and fun. Amen.

DAY 2

# SO WHAT'S FAITH?

Faith means being sure of the things we hope for and knowing that something is real even if we do not see it.

—HEBREWS 11:1 NCV

The other day the Brave Girls were talking about how hard being brave and living for God can be. Hope pointed out that to be brave, you first have to have a strong faith in God because it's His power that gives us the strength to do brave things. That made so much sense! But then Gracie asked what *faith* really means. Everyone looked at me—it's my name, after all! But I wasn't exactly sure.

So I asked my mom and dad. This is how they explained it to me:

Faith is more than a warm, fuzzy feeling. It's more than simply believing in God. And it's definitely not just trusting Him without thinking about it either. Faith is *knowing* God is real by looking at all the evidence—like all the wonders of nature. Faith is also *trusting* God to keep His promises—because of all the promises He has already kept in His Word. Faith is also *acting* like God is real by being the person He wants you to be.

Faith is a lot of things, but it all starts with believing. And He gives us so many reasons to believe! Here's one: go outside and pick a flower, a leaf, or even a blade of grass. Do you see all those details? No way they just happened by accident! Now look around at all the flowers, leaves, trees, animals, stars, and people. Each one was designed by God, the Creator of all! You can have faith in Him!

## A BRAVE GIRL'S PRAYER

Lord, open my eyes to see just how real You are! And help me live like I truly trust You. Amen.

Glory

# LIVE IT

*If we are not faithful, [God] will still be faithful, because He must be true to who He is.*

—2 TIMOTHY 2:13 NCV

So if faith is *knowing* God is real and *trusting* Him to keep His promises, what does it mean to be faithful? And how can that be fun?

First of all, being faithful means to be . . . well . . . full of faith. Okay, so you're probably thinking, *Glory, that's not the most helpful of definitions!* Maybe this will make it clearer: being faithful is putting our faith into action. It's getting up every day and living like we really do believe all God's promises and like we really do want follow Him.

Being faithful looks like . . .

- **not worrying** because you know God has promised to give you everything you need.

- **trusting God** to help you do what's right, even when no one else is doing it.

- **forgiving others** because God forgives you.

- **being kind and encouraging** because that's what God asks you to do.

- **serving others** because even Jesus came to serve.

- **finding reasons to smile**, no matter what else is happening, because God loves you.

A faithful life is a beautiful life . . . to God and to everyone around you! And one of the most beautiful things about God is that He is always faithful to us—even when we forget to be faithful to Him.

## A BRAVE GIRL'S PRAYER

Lord, show me how I can put my faith into action today. Amen.

Clothes to Donate

# FOOD + FRIENDS = FUN

Then he told the people to sit down on the grass. He took the five loaves and the two fish and, looking to heaven, he thanked God for the food.

—MATTHEW 14:19 NCV

The only thing better than being outside is being outside with my friends. Add some food, and we're sure to have a fun time! So when I learned about this amazing picnic Jesus had with a few thousand of His friends, that gave me a *great* idea.

You see, Jesus' picnic started when a crowd followed Him into the countryside. Jesus talked to them all day, teaching them about God. Soon it was the end of the day, and people were getting hungry. They were far away from the towns, and it wasn't as if they could order a pizza. Plus, Jesus wasn't done hanging out with everyone!

While the disciples wondered what to do, a boy offered to share his meal. So Jesus told everyone to sit down on the grass. Then He prayed to God, thanking Him for the food. And God miraculously made that meal enough to feed *all* the people. They even had leftovers!

That's when I had my idea: I would invite all the Brave Girls out to the farm for a picnic. And we could each invite someone else to share in the fun. Maybe we would even have a chance to tell them about Jesus' picnic!

You can plan a picnic too. Invite your best friends and some new friends. Include the new girl, the girl who always seems to be left out, or someone you'd simply like to get to know better. And don't forget to thank God for the food!

## A BRAVE GIRL'S PRAYER

Holy Father, thank You for food— and for friends to share it with. Amen.

# HOW TO PLAN THE PERFECT PICNIC

Food just tastes better when you share it with friends—especially on a picnic! You can host a picnic with a little easy planning.

**PREPARATION TIME: 45 MINUTES**

## MATERIALS

blanket, large tablecloth, or old sheet

bag, basket, or cooler to carry your food

ice or ice packs

your favorite drinks

plates, cups, napkins, and utensils

cold main dish, such as sandwiches or fried chicken

finger foods, such as fruit, veggies and dip, chips, or cheese and crackers

something sweet for dessert

trash bag

bug spray and sunscreen

equipment for outdoor games, such as Frisbee, kickball, or badminton

> For a different spin on a sandwich, make Tortilla Roll-Ups.
> Using one tortilla per person, spread your favorite savory cream cheese on the tortilla. Then cover the tortilla in deli meat and sliced cheese. For some crunch, add lettuce. Roll up tightly. Slice into discs.

## STEPS

1. Decide when and where to have your picnic. You'll want a shady spot with room to spread out. Invite your friends at least one week before your chosen date.

2. Plan the menu, and ask an adult to take you to the store to buy the food and supplies.

3. On the day of the picnic, prepare your food and pack it into the basket or cooler. Be sure to pack the cold things with plenty of ice or ice packs.

4. Gather your food, supplies, and friends, and head to the picnic spot. Spread out your blanket or sheet.

5. When everyone is ready to eat, lay out the food, drinks, plates, and utensils.

6. Give thanks to God for your food, your friends, and fun times together.

7. Eat and play!

8. Before you leave, pick up any trash. Try to leave the spot better than you found it.

### A PICNIC PRAYER

Lord, we thank You for this food, for our friendships, and for all the fun and blessings You pour into our lives. Amen.

Honor

# TO THE RESCUE

Do not forget to do good to others, and share with them, because such sacrifices please God.

—HEBREWS 13:16 NCV

My parents call me their "little rescuer." That's because I'm always rescuing lost and hurt animals. If I see an animal in need, I just have to help.

Mostly, I think, my parents are happy that's who I am—well, except perhaps for that time my mom went to take a shower and found a turtle swimming in the tub. And I guess my dad wasn't thrilled when I used his hair clippers to shave the matted hair off that stray dog. But other than that . . .

You see, I believe God wants us to take care of His creatures. That's the job He gave Adam and Eve in the garden (Genesis 2:15). And Matthew 10:29 tells us that He knows what happens to every single sparrow. So He'll know if I've tried to help one or not, right?

But animals aren't the only ones who need rescuing. People do too. That's why I've made it my mission to rescue someone or something at least once every week—more often, if I can. Will you join me?

It doesn't have to be a huge thing either. If your parents are overwhelmed by work and chores, do a load of laundry or dishes. An older neighbor might need help sweeping off their steps or bringing in the mail. Or maybe you could tutor a friend who is struggling with a class that you're great in. Take a look around: Who can you rescue today?

## A BRAVE GIRL'S PRAYER

Lord, make me a rescuer. Use me to rescue someone today. Amen.

*Gracie*

DAY 6

# ROCKIN' PRAISES

You will live in joy and peace. The mountains and hills will burst into song, and the trees of the field will clap their hands!

—ISAIAH 55:12 NLT

Everybody has their "thing." For Hope, it's sports. For Honor, it's animals. Glory loves all things beautiful, and Faith is happiest when she's painting. For me, though, I've discovered that my "thing" is music. I love listening to it, singing it, and dancing to it.

So when I stumbled across this verse in Isaiah, you can imagine how happy I was to discover that music is one of God's "things" too. Check it out: "The mountains and hills will burst into song, and the trees of the field will clap their hands!" Wouldn't you love to see—and hear—that?

Jesus even says that if people don't praise Him, the rocks will do it (Luke 19:40)! Talk about a rock concert! (And yeah, that was a terrible joke, but I'll bet it made you smile!)

Take a walk outside today and listen to what God's creation is singing. What are some of the different kinds of music you hear? Are the birds chirping? Is the wind whistling through the trees? Maybe you hear ocean waves or a creek babbling. Add your own song and "rock out" with some praises to the One who taught the world to sing!

**A BRAVE GIRL'S PRAYER**

Lord, teach me to hear Your creation sing Your praises! Amen.

17

# ENCOURAGEMENT ROCKS!

Since encouraging others really rocks, why not make some rocks that encourage others? Create a single stone or a whole rock garden.

TIME: 1 HOUR, PLUS EXTRA DRY TIME

## MATERIALS

flat stones

acrylic craft paint

paintbrush

permanent marker

sealer, such as Mod Podge (optional)

## STEPS

1. Choose a flat, smooth stone. It can be any size, but one that fits nicely in your hand works best. To help the paint stick, wash the stone with warm, soapy water. Dry thoroughly.

2. Paint one side of the stone. You can paint it a solid color or create a design. If your stone is dark, you may need to do more than one coat of paint. Let the stone dry between coats. (You can paint both sides, if you wish. Just paint one side first, let it dry, and then paint the other side.)

3. When the paint is dry, use your permanent marker to write your message on the stone. It could be an encouraging word, such as *love*, *joy*, or *peace*. It could be a symbol, such as a heart or cross. Or it could be a Bible verse reference, such as John 3:16 or Psalm 23.

4. If you want your stone to last longer in outside weather, cover it with a layer of Mod Podge and let it dry. (Don't worry—it will dry clear!)

5. Tuck a rock in your pocket, give one to a friend, or leave one in a random spot to be discovered.

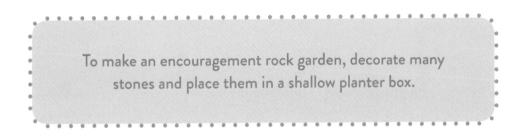

To make an encouragement rock garden, decorate many stones and place them in a shallow planter box.

DAY 7

# LOOK UP AND LOOK OUT

Do not be interested only in your own life, but
be interested in the lives of others.

—PHILIPPIANS 2:4 NCV

My mom has a saying. She actually has a lot of sayings, but this one is really good. Whenever I'm having a tough day and I'm starting to feel sorry for myself, my mom will say, "When things are looking down, that's a good time to look up and look out."

By "look up," she means I should look up to the skies, to the clouds, to the sunshine. Because when I look up at all that God has made, I remember how big and strong and powerful He really is. And I realize that no matter how big my troubles might seem, God is so much bigger. He can help me handle anything!

"Look out" means I need to look out at the world around me and see who I can help. When I get busy helping my neighbor bring in her groceries or teaching my little brothers to catch a football, I quickly forget to feel sorry for myself.

Like my mom always says, you don't have to wait for a bad day to look up and look out. Go ahead and give it a try today. Look up and look out . . . what do you see?

## A BRAVE GIRL'S PRAYER

Holy Lord, help me look up and look out each day. I want to live for You and for others. Amen.

# TRUE FRIENDS

A true friend sticks by you like family.
—PROVERBS 18:24 THE MESSAGE

Hope, Honor, Faith, and Gracie are my best friends because they are true friends. We stand by each other and stick up for each other. We laugh and cry together. We help and encourage each other. I don't know what I would have done without the Brave Girls when my parents got a divorce. They really pulled me through that terrible time.

True friends are a beautiful treasure. And like any treasure, you'll probably have to search to find them. I've learned—sometimes the hard way—that people will *say* they're your friend when they really aren't. Some are friendly people you share a class or a neighborhood with. Others pretend to be your friend when they're with you; then they act like an enemy behind your back. And who needs that?

A true friend is more than someone to have fun with; she's someone you can lean on when times are tough. She doesn't just *say* she is your friend; she lives out her friendship by listening to what you say and sticking up for you, even when you're not around. She doesn't ignore you or use your secrets for gossip. A true friend shares her thoughts, her time, and her heart. She prays for you and is even willing to gently tell you when you are wrong.

The secret to finding a true friend is to first be one yourself. If you need an example, follow Jesus—He's the truest friend of all. Who can you be a true friend to today?

## A BRAVE GIRL'S PRAYER

Lord, please bless me with a true friend, and teach me to be a true friend in return. Amen.

# QUICK & EASY FRIENDSHIP BRACELET

TIME: 30 MINUTES

## MATERIALS

embroidery floss in 3 colors

## TOOLS

scissors

tape

flat surface, such as a clipboard or tabletop

This craft is perfect for group events. Make bracelets with your besties at your next party or sleepover.

## STEPS

1. Cut a 32-inch (82-cm) piece of each color of floss.

2. Gather the three strings together and tie a knot about 3 inches (8 cm) from the end.

3. Tape the ends closest to the knot to the flat surface.

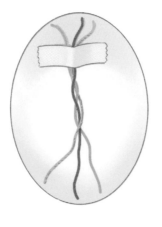

4. Start with the strand on the left. Wrap it around your left thumb, and cross it over the other two strings to make a number 4 shape.

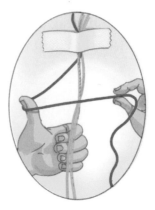

**5.** Loop the strand under the other two strands and then pull it through the middle of the 4. Remove your thumb, and tug the strand up to form a snug knot.

**6.** Repeat steps 4 and 5 until you want to switch to another color.

**7.** To change colors, move the strand of the new color next to your left hand. Move the other colors to the right. Repeat steps 4 and 5 until you're ready to change colors again.

**8.** Keep tying knots until you reach about 3 inches (8 cm) from the end of the strings. Tie all the strings in a knot. Trim off the extra thread at each end, leaving about a half inch (2 cm).

**9.** Tie around your wrist or the wrist of a friend.

Experiment using different numbers of strands—you can use as many as you'd like!

DAY 9

# THE POTTER AND THE CLAY POT

*"You are like the clay in the potter's hands."*

—JEREMIAH 18:6 ICB

Because I'm homeschooled, my sister and I have Bible lessons as part of our homework. I don't mind; it just means I get to learn even more about God.

Today's lesson was from the book of Jeremiah. It was about a potter and a lump of clay. The potter was shaping the clay to be something useful, but something went wrong. Instead of throwing it out, though, the potter simply started over. He squished it all up again and shaped the clay until it was just the way he wanted it. That potter is like God, and we are the clay He's forming.

God made us to be part of His kingdom, but our sin can mess things up. God doesn't give up on us though. He keeps working on us and shaping us to be exactly what He wants us to be. That part might not always be fun because sometimes God uses troubles and struggles to shape us. Even in those times, we can still know that He's always working on us to make us more like Jesus.

Do you know someone who's having a tough time? Make them a simple gift to remind them that God is still working in their lives. Take a terra-cotta clay pot, and use a hot glue gun to decorate it with shells, scraps of lace or twine, or even bark. (Be sure to check with a grown-up for how to use a glue gun.) Then tuck a pretty flower or a handful of candies inside, along with a note, for a pretty pick-me-up gift.

## A BRAVE GIRL'S PRAYER

Lord, thank You for all the ways You work in my life to make me more like You. Amen.

# SCOOCH OVER

"Come, follow me," Jesus said.
—MATTHEW 4:19 NIV

These days I can't imagine not being a part of the Brave Girls. They are so special and such good friends. I still remember the first time I met them in Sunday school.

You see, my family had just moved to town. And while we hardly ever went to church where we lived before, my parents thought this move to a new town would be a good time to start. Everyone was very friendly during the church service, but I'm not gonna lie, walking into that Sunday school class all by myself was so hard. And then, when they started going over the lesson, I quickly figured out that these kids all knew *a lot* more about the Bible than I did. What if I said something completely wrong or even stupid? I just wanted to slink under the table and hide.

When class was over, I was ready to run. But Faith, Hope, Honor, and Glory were standing by the door. Before I could escape, they opened up their circle and pulled me in. It was the start of a great friendship with them—and a great friendship with God.

Here's the thing I learned from all that: we need to open our circles and pull people in. Life is hard enough without being left out. So invite people to join you at church. Scooch over and make room at the lunch table. Pull people into your group of friends in the hallway at school. Find someone to include today.

### A BRAVE GIRL'S PRAYER

Lord, show me who I need to make some room for today. Amen.

Hope

1

# A JOYFUL NOISE

Shout to the Lord, all the earth; break out in praise and sing for joy!

—PSALM 98:4 NLT

Gracie is the singer in our group. She's amazing! When she sings, people stop whatever they're doing and listen.

As for me? Well, let's just say there are a lot of buckets on my family's farm, and they can all carry a tune better than I can. Don't get me wrong—I'm not putting myself down. There are lots of things I'm good at. Singing just isn't one of them.

The thing is, I love to sing. I especially love to sing about God and how awesome He is. For a long time though, I wouldn't sing out in church or youth group because I was afraid of being compared to Gracie. Then one day I realized I wasn't singing *for* the people around me. I was singing *to* God. He doesn't care how I sound. God loves to hear His children sing to Him.

Now I sing to God all the time. I know a major recording contract isn't in my future. And I'm okay with that. (It might be for Gracie someday. Seriously, she's awesome!) But God has put a song in my heart, and it's fun to sing it out!

Sometimes I look at all the things God created right here on our farm, and I'm so amazed that I make up my own song of praise. Why don't you give it a try? Take a look around you and make up a song about how awesome God is.

## A BRAVE GIRL'S PRAYER

God, help me not to be afraid to sing out about Your goodness. I want to praise You all the time. Amen.

# STICK TOGETHER

*No one has ever seen God, but if we love each other,
God lives in us, and His love is made perfect in us.*

—1 JOHN 4:12 NCV

Honor

The Brave Girls and I like to say that we stick together—and this last weekend we *really* did! It was such a beautiful, sunny day that I decided to try out a science experiment on my friends. And no, I didn't turn their hair green or anything like that! You see, I had built a solar oven, but I hadn't tested it yet. *S'mores*, I thought, *would be the perfect test for my little oven.*

The s'mores were amazing! The marshmallows were so gooey that soon we were all sticking together! But even more wonderful than the s'mores was the time we spent just laughing and talking together in the sunshine.

Some people think that you have to be reading your Bible or praying or doing a service project to be doing something spiritual. But sometimes living for God simply means spending time with the godly friends He's given you. The Bible says that one way we can experience God's love is by loving each other. When I hang out with the Brave Girls—especially when there are marshmallows and sunshine—I can't help but be blown away by God's love for me.

How about you? Do you have godly friends who show you a little bit of God's amazing love? Plan to get together soon and just hang out. If you're needing some new friends, or some better friends, reach out to a girl at church you don't know well and invite her to make s'mores. Your new friend just might stick!

## A BRAVE GIRL'S PRAYER

Lord, thank You for Your great love and for friendship. Help me find friends who want to live for You. Amen.

# SOLAR OVEN S'MORES

All you need is a sunny day and this make-it-yourself
solar oven to enjoy some yummy s'mores.

TIME: 30 MINUTES TO ASSEMBLE OVEN,
      30 MINUTES TO PREHEAT,
      30–60 MINUTES TO COOK S'MORES

## MATERIALS

1 large shoe box, at least 11 inches
    (28 cm) wide and deep

aluminum foil

clear plastic wrap

glue stick

tape

ruler or stick, about 12 inches
    (30 cm) long

9- or 10-inch (23–25 cm)
    aluminum pie pan

chocolate bars, graham crackers,
    and large marshmallows

## TOOLS

box cutter or X-Acto knife (use with a grown-up's help)

## STEPS

1. Use the box cutter or X-Acto knife to cut a three-sided flap out of the top of the box. Leave at least a 1-inch (3-cm) border around the flap.

2. Use the glue stick to cover the inside of the box and the underside of the flap with aluminum foil. Try to keep the foil smooth and flat, like a mirror.

3. With the flap open, tape a sheet of plastic wrap under the hole in the box lid. Open the entire lid, and tape another layer of plastic wrap under the hole from the bottom side. This will keep the heat in and the bugs out!

4. Prop the flap open with the stick or ruler. You may need to use tape to keep it in place.

5. Keeping the flap open, place the oven in direct sunlight for at least 30 minutes. Turn it so that the sun reflects into the oven.

6. Break 2 graham crackers in half and place the 4 halves in the pie pan. Add a marshmallow on top of each. Don't add the chocolate or top cracker yet.

7. Place the pan in the oven. Close the lid (the part with the plastic wrap), but keep the flap open. Cook until the marshmallows are squishy—about 30 to 60 minutes.

8. Top with a square of chocolate and a graham cracker. Squeeze together, and enjoy!

DAY 13

# LISTEN UP

Always be willing to listen and slow to speak.

—JAMES 1:19 ICB

Do you know someone who loves to talk? Who can chatter away all day long? Well . . . that's me. *Especially* if I'm talking about fashion and shopping.

But the other day I was chattering away about this fabulous coat I saw when I noticed that even though Hope was listening very nicely, she wasn't enjoying the conversation as much as I was. That's when I realized that maybe I needed to do a bit less talking and a bit more listening. When I asked Hope about the new baby chicks on her farm, she got so excited telling me all about them. And I had fun listening to her stories about the chicks' adventures.

There are times when listening is fun, like hearing Hope's stories. There are other times when it's not as fun, like when my friends are hurting or sad. Those are the times when listening is most important though. I know I was so grateful that the Brave Girls listened while I poured out everything I was worried about when my parents split up. And the hugs they gave were a huge help too!

While listening may not seem like you're doing much, it's actually one of the most wonderful ways to serve others. To be a good listener, you'll need to practice. Try these three tips: Stop whatever else you're doing. Look people in the eye. And focus on what they're saying—not on what you want to say next! Who can you listen to today?

## A BRAVE GIRL'S PRAYER

Lord, teach me to listen more and talk less—especially with You! Amen.

# GIVE IT A TRY

If anyone is in Christ, he is a new creation; old things have passed away; behold, all things have become new.
—2 CORINTHIANS 5:17 NKJV

I have a confession to make: when it comes to trying new things, well, that's not really my thing. I like to stick with what I already know, like my art and my Brave Girls friends.

Then one night in youth group, we talked about how Jesus made each of us a new creation. As an artist, that verse jumped out at me because I love to create new things. That's when I started thinking that maybe part of being a new creation means not getting stuck in doing the same old things—even if they're good things.

So I decided to try something new. I went to art camp for *two whole weeks*! At first I was worried about being away from home for so long. But once I got there and started trying some of the different ways of creating art, I had a blast! I made new friends, and I even learned how to put verses from the Bible in my art. Trying something new gave me a different way to share God with others.

You don't have to go away to camp to try something new. You can do something today—right now!—like making your own Bible art. It's easy, and I'll show you how. Go ahead. Give it a try!

## A BRAVE GIRL'S PRAYER

God, is there something new You would like me to try? Please show me what it is, and give me the courage to go for it. Amen.

# A WORD OF ART

The words of the Bible are beautiful in the way they speak to our hearts.
Make them beautiful to see as well by turning them into art.

**TIME: 30 MINUTES, A LITTLE LONGER IF YOU USE WATERCOLORS**

## MATERIALS

1 favorite Bible verse, such as Psalm 51:10, Psalm 139:14, Isaiah 41:10, Philippians 4:13, or Matthew 28:20

1 sheet heavy paper or cardstock (in a light color)

colored pencils or watercolors

1 pencil

1 black or dark permanent marker

## STEPS

1. Using a pencil, write the Bible verse on the paper.

2. Once you're happy with your lettering, darken the pencil so that it will show through the paint.

3. Lightly color the entire sheet of paper using either colored pencils or watercolors. You can color the paper in all one color, blend colors together, or draw a picture or scene. Or simply doodle. Just be sure you can still see your pencil marks.

4. If you use watercolors, let the paint dry completely.

5. Use the permanent marker to trace over your pencil marks.

Your "Word of Art" is now ready to be given as a gift or kept for yourself as a beautiful reminder of God's Word.

He rescued me because
He delighted in me.
Psalm 18:19

Gracie

# WHEN YOU FAIL AT FUN

THERE is one THING I always do: I forget the THings that are past.
I try as hard as I can to reach the goal that is before me.
—PHILIPPIANS 3:13 ICB

I can still remember the first time I tried to sing a solo. I was absolutely terrified—I had so many butterflies in my stomach that I thought I might be sick!

I loved singing when I was by myself or in a group, but I wasn't sure I could do it in front of others. What if I forgot the words? Or hit all the wrong notes? Or tripped going up onto the stage? Singing in front of people was a huge risk for me. But you know what? It worked out great.

There have been other things I've tried, though, that didn't work out so well—like that time I tried painting with Faith. Talk about disasters! Even sweet Faith couldn't help but laugh at my attempts. At first I got a little upset because I really had tried so hard. But then I looked at my painting and realized . . . yeah, it was pretty funny-looking!

What do you do if you try your hardest, give it your best shot, do all you can do . . . and it still completely flops? Well, you pick yourself up, dust yourself off, and maybe even laugh a little. Then you congratulate yourself for doing a great job at figuring out one thing that *isn't* your thing. Seriously, just check that off the list and move on to the next thing. Don't let failure keep you from discovering all the amazing things you *can* do!

## A BRAVE GIRL'S PRAYER

Holy Father, I know I can't be good at everything. When I fail, help me learn from it . . . and learn to laugh at my mistakes. Amen.

DAY 16

# GOOD TO GET AWAY

Jesus said, "Let's go off by ourselves to a quiet place and rest awhile."

—MARK 6:31 NLT

I am so excited! My best friends—the Brave Girls—are on their way over to have a sleepover. We always have the best time when we're together. Sometimes we play games or watch a movie. Tonight my dad is taking us all on a hayride around the farm after dark, and my mom has picked up all the ingredients we need to make our own pizzas.

The best part, though, is that I'll get to just be with my friends. We've all had some hard times lately, and we're all trying to figure out this growing-up thing. And I'm sure we'll talk about all that a little, but I'm looking forward to just being together. It's good for me—for all of us—to get away from the pressures of school and chores, and to just hang out and be silly together for a little while.

Jesus did that too. Not the hayride and pizza part, of course. But sometimes He got away from the crowds and all the pressures to just be with His closest friends. If even Jesus needed to do that, I know that I do too! Plan to get away with your friends soon. Maybe for a sleepover, an afternoon in the park, or a movie at the mall. Getting away with your friends is more than just good fun; it's good for you too!

## A BRAVE GIRL'S PRAYER

Dear God, thank You for my friends and for the chance to get away together. Amen.

# PITa PIZZaS

TIME: 15 MINUTES

MAKES: 6 PIZZAS

## INGREDIENTS

6 pita breads

1½ cups (350 ml) pizza sauce

1½ cups (170 g) shredded mozzarella cheese

toppings, such as pepperoni, ham, pineapple, peppers, olives—whatever you
  like best!

## TOOLS

baking sheet

spoon

oven or toaster oven (ask a grown-up for help)

This recipe is perfect for parties, sleepovers, and other group gatherings because each person can choose her own favorite toppings.

## STEPS

1. Preheat the oven or toaster oven to 400 degrees Fahrenheit (205 degrees C).

2. Spread pizza sauce over each pita.

3. Sprinkle each pita with cheese.

4. Add toppings.

5. Bake for 5–7 minutes or until the cheese is melted and bubbly.

DAY 17

# SOMETHING TO MAKE YOU SMILE

I pray that you and all God's holy people will have the power to understand the greatness of Christ's love—how wide and how long and how high and how deep that love is.

—EPHESIANS 3:18 NCV

What's the absolute tallest thing you can think of? A skyscraper? Mount Everest? The distance from the earth to the moon? How about the widest thing? The Grand Canyon? The ocean? The universe? What's the longest thing or the deepest thing? No matter what the tallest, widest, longest, or deepest things you can think of might be, God's love for you stretches higher and wider, lasts longer, and goes deeper than any of those things.

Go on. Just try not to smile at that.

I don't know about you, but there are some days when I have to search for a reason to smile. Even though I've mostly gotten used to my new school after I skipped a grade, there are still hard days. Sometimes the other kids are being difficult. Other times I don't do as well as I think I should on a test. Or maybe it's just one of those days when everything seems to go wrong.

That's why I keep Ephesians 3:18 written right on the front of my notebook. That way, it's always there to remind me of the very best reason to smile: God loves me!

Is there a verse that makes you smile? That cheers you up on tough days? Write it on the front of your notebook (or wherever you'll see it often). Every time you see it, let it remind you to smile!

## A BRAVE GIRL'S PRAYER

Dear God, on days when I'm having trouble finding a reason to smile, remind me of just how wide and deep and tall and long Your love for me is. Amen.

# BETTER TOGETHER

Two people are better than one, because they
get more done by working together.

—ECCLESIASTES 4:9 NCV

I love Brave Girls sleepovers! Last time was at my house, and we played games and ate all kinds of yummy snacks. We even made our own pizzas! And of course, we stayed up so late laughing and talking—that's always the best part.

But in the morning I looked around, and the house was a mess! You see, one of my mom's rules for sleepovers is that my friends are always welcome, but the mess must be cleaned up right away. And let's just say there was a *lot* to clean up this time. Turns out making your own pizzas can really wreck a kitchen.

Just as I was starting to get bummed about spending the next couple hours cleaning, Faith walked into the kitchen with a bunch of dirty dishes. Then Glory squirted dish soap into the sink and turned on the hot water. Honor grabbed a trash bag and started tossing stuff in while Gracie scrubbed the counters. We turned on some tunes and danced and sang and giggled. Then we *might* have had to also clean up a bit of water from splashing each other with the soap bubbles. Before I knew it, we were done—and the cleaning had actually been fun!

The next time you see a friend facing a big, yucky chore, don't slip away. Turn on some tunes and join in. Two (or more!) working together is so much better— you'll get the job done faster and have fun too!

## A BRAVE GIRL'S PRAYER

God, thank You for the joy of working with friends! Amen.

Glory

# SOAR ABOVE THE STORMS

"Look at the birds in the air. They don't plant or harvest or store food in barns, but your heavenly Father feeds them. And you know that you are worth much more than the birds."
—MATTHEW 6:26 NCV

Birds are one of the most beautiful and amazing of God's creations, or at least they are to me. Imagine something so tiny being able to fly so high, to dart in and out of clouds, and to soar up above the storms. I'd like to be able to do that—to fly high above the earth, without any worries or fears. And wouldn't it be wonderful to use the clouds like your very own playground, bouncing from one white puff to the next? Then to be able to soar up above all the storms and troubles—now that's something I'd *really* like to be able to do.

Those birds don't seem to have a worry in the world. Perhaps that's because they know their heavenly Father takes care of them. Just like I know that God takes care of me. After all, He tells me that I am worth much more than the birds. And by the way—so are you!

Remind yourself of God's love and care by making a super-easy bird feeder. Just tie a string around a pine cone. Mix together equal parts of oats and peanut butter. Spread it over the pine cone and roll it in birdseed. Then hang the feeder where you can see it. Each time you see a bird, remember to praise the God who takes care of you both.

## A BRAVE GIRL'S PRAYER

Lord, I praise You for the way You always take care of me. Amen.

Gracie

# NOT-SO-LITTLE LITTLE THINGS

Jesus went everywhere doing good.

—ACTS 10:38 NCV

Every time I go to church, I learn something new about Jesus. Like how He stopped a storm just by telling it to be quiet (Mark 4:39), how He helped blind people see and deaf people hear (Matthew 15:30), and even how He raised Lazarus from the *dead* (John 11:43). Jesus did some really big, amazing, and miraculous things in the Bible.

But Jesus did little things too. And while those things weren't really miracles, they were pretty special to the people He did them for. Like that outcast Samaritan woman He talked to by the well (John 4:1–30), the friend He wept with (John 11:35), and those kids He hugged (Matthew 19:14–15).

I'll never get a storm to stop by telling it to hush. I won't ever heal blind people so they can see. And I definitely won't be raising anybody back to life again. But I *can* do the same little things that Jesus did.

I can hug a child. I can cry with a friend. I can tell someone about Jesus. Because even though these things might seem small, they're really huge to that child, that friend, and that person who decides to believe in Him.

What not-so-little little thing can you do today?

## A BRAVE GIRL'S PRAYER

Dear God, help me share a little bit of Your goodness everywhere I go today. Amen.

# RANDOM KINDNESS SCAVENGER HUNT

How many random acts of kindness can you do? Gather your friends at a mall or shopping center and divide into two groups. Give each group a copy of the following list. Set a time limit, and at the end of that time, the group that has checked off the most items wins. Of course, in this game, no one loses!

- ☐ Smile at someone and get a smile in return.
- ☐ Thank three people, such as a waiter, a cashier, and a police officer.
- ☐ Throw away a piece of litter.
- ☐ Hold the door for someone.
- ☐ Help carry something.
- ☐ Share something.
- ☐ Give something away.
- ☐ Leave a "Jesus cares about you" sticky note on a mirror.
- ☐ Encourage someone.
- ☐ Give a sincere compliment to someone.
- ☐ Leave a secret gift, such as a plastic animal or a note.
- ☐ Pray with someone.
- ☐ Pray for someone you don't know.
- ☐ Text a friend hello.
- ☐ Listen to a praise song—and sing along!
- ☐ Memorize a verse and recite it for your friends.
- ☐ Find three unusual things to thank God for.
- ☐ Clean up a mess.
- ☐ Write a thank-you note to the person who drove you today.
- ☐ Say "I love you" to a close friend or family member.

Faith

# WHEN FUN ISN'T FUN

I'm not trying to win the approval of people, but of God.

—GALATIANS 1:10 NLT

Do you ever try too hard to fit in? Do you sometimes go overboard to make sure you please everyone around you?

I definitely do! My people-pleasing especially trips me up with the people closest to me. It's honestly easier for me to say no to the bad stuff or to the people I'm not close with than it is to say no to my friends. Like the time I went to the water park with Hope when we first met. She really wanted to go down the big waterslide. The thing is, heights really scare me. And I'm not the greatest swimmer. But I wanted Hope to like me, so I went.

Going down that slide was even more horrible than I had imagined. I swallowed so much water, and the lifeguard had to fish me out. I was so embarrassed!

Fortunately, Hope figured out the problem. She actually scolded me for not telling her that I didn't want to go down the slide. After that, we headed over to ride the waves in the wave pool—something we *both* like to do.

Remember this: even though it's important to try new things, it's okay to say some things just aren't for you. We all want to fit in, especially with our friends. But we shouldn't let people-pleasing pressure us into doing things we don't want to do—even good things that our friends think are fun. There will always be something you can both enjoy together.

## A BRAVE GIRL'S PRAYER

Lord, remind me that one way to please You is to be true to who You made me to be. Amen.

Honor

# 100 THOUSAND MILLION AND COUNTING

He counts the stars and names each one.

—PSALM 147:4 NCV

One of the coolest things about science is the way it proves how awesome God is. Like the other day I learned the most amazing thing about the stars. Did you know that scientists now think there are more than one hundred thousand million stars in our Milky Way galaxy? And they're still counting! Even more amazing, they believe there are millions and millions of other galaxies in the universe. The most amazing thing of all is that God made each and every one of those stars and placed them exactly where He wanted them. Scientists can't count the stars, but God can—and He even calls each one of them by its own name!

Now this is the part I really love: the same God who counts and names all those stars knows our names too—mine and yours and everyone else's who has ever lived. And God doesn't just know our names; He knows our worries, our fears, our strengths, and our weaknesses. He even knows the things that make us smile—and He fills up our lives with them.

So here's a challenge for you: try to count all the things that make you smile today. Even on the worst days—if you look for them—you'll find that there are too many to count.

## A BRAVE GIRL'S PRAYER

Lord, thank You for filling my life with things that make me smile. Open my eyes to see them all! Amen.

DAY 23

# GO PLaY!

The streets of the city will be filled with boys and girls at play.

—ZECHARIAH 8:5 NLT

If you hang around *some* Christians, you might get the idea that serving God is all about work, work, work, and then some more work. And yeah, there are things God wants you to do for Him and for all the people He loves.

But if you just take a look around this world, you'll see that there is so much more to loving and praising God. After all, He didn't have to make trees so wonderfully climbable (I might be making that word up!) or hills so roll-down-able (I'm *definitely* making that word up!). God didn't have to make puddles to jump over or creeks to splash through. But He made all those things and more! There is no playground we could ever build that would be as amazing as the one God created in this world.

Enjoying God's wonderful world is one way we can praise Him for His creation. And you don't have to live on a farm like me—just go outside and play! Seriously, you're not too grown-up. In fact, you're never too old to play. So turn off the screens, grab a friend or a few, and go outside and play!

One of my favorite games is still good old-fashioned hide-and-seek. Make it more of a challenge by setting a time limit for finding everyone or by declaring that a hiding spot can be used only once for the whole game.

### A BRAVE GIRL'S PRAYER

God, help me remember that I'm never too old to praise You with the joy of playing in Your creation. Amen.

Glory

DAY 24

# FIND THE FUN

Everything you say and everything you do should all be done for Jesus your Lord. And in all you do, give thanks to God the Father through Jesus.

—COLOSSIANS 3:17 ICB

You've probably figured out that I love clothes—shopping for them, wearing them, and even drawing my own designs for them. But one thing I do *not* love is washing them! I know it has to be done. Otherwise, well . . . ick.

My mom says I'm growing up, and I need to learn to do my own laundry. She's really busy these days, and it would be good to help her out (and have clean clothes without having to bug her!), but still . . . ick.

I was complaining to my friends about it when Gracie said, "Glory, you've gotta do it, so make it fun." My first thought was *Puh-lease. Laundry could never be fun!* But then I thought about it.

First I made a list of the things I like about laundry. (It was short!) Number one, I like all my clothes being clean, so I can choose whatever I feel like wearing most that day. Number two, I like the smell of clothes fresh out of the dryer. Next, I decided I would do something fun while the clothes are in the machines, like sketching new designs, texting with my friends, or baking cookies. Then, after it's all put away, I treat myself to a bath with extra bubbles. Now I almost look forward to laundry. Yeah, *almost*. But it's a *lot* better.

If you've got a chore you really don't like, find a way to add some fun. Figure out one thing you like about it, add something fun (like turning on some tunes), and then treat yourself to something special when the chore is done.

## A BRAVE GIRL'S PRAYER

Lord, teach me to find a little joy in everything I have to do. Amen.

# HOW TO DO LAUNDRY

Knowing how to wash clothes is a skill you'll need your whole life—and it will be a huge help. (The first few times, ask a grown-up to help you sort the clothes and teach you how the washer and dryer work.)

## MATERIALS

dirty clothes

laundry detergent

stain remover spray

fabric softener liquid or dryer sheets

## TOOLS

washer

dryer

hangers

## STEPS

1. First, sort the clothes into piles of things that get washed the same way. Start by making piles of light-colored clothes and dark-colored clothes. Check the tags on each item, and make separate piles for anything that says "hand wash" or "dry clean only." Make separate piles for towels and sheets.

2. Check all the pockets and remove anything inside them.

3. Spray stain remover on any spots.

4. Put one sorted pile into the washer and add the laundry detergent. If you're using liquid softener, add that now too. Check the labels on the bottles to see how much detergent and softener to add.

5. Use the guide on the washer (and the tags on the clothes) to help you choose the right

wash cycle. Be sure to ask a grown-up too. Turn on the washer. Set a timer to remind you to come back when the load is done.

6. When the wash cycle is done, move the clothes to the dryer. Be sure to remove any clothes with tags that say "hang dry" or "dry flat." Clean out the lint trap.

7. Choose the best dryer cycle for the clothes you're drying. (Again, check with a grown-up. Also check the guide on the machine and the clothing tags for instructions.) If you're using a dryer sheet, toss one in now. Turn on the dryer, and set a timer.

8. Hang up or lay out any clothes that need to be air-dried.

9. While the first load is drying, put the second load in the washing machine. Follow all the steps again for that load.

10. When the clothes are dry, take them out right away so there are fewer wrinkles. Hang up any clothes that go in the closets. Fold the rest.

11. Deliver all the clothes to the room they belong in, and put them away.

Read the care tags on the inside of clothes to learn any special instructions.

**Hand wash:** Wash with laundry detergent in a sink. Or use your machine's hand-wash cycle if it has one.

**Dry clean only:** Ask an adult. Sometimes you can hand wash these items. But some things actually need to be taken to the dry cleaners.

**Hang dry:** Wash in the machine, then hang in an open space until completely dry.

**Dry flat:** Spread out the item on a towel or drying rack, and smooth out any wrinkles.

Congratulations! You've done the laundry—and been a huge help to your family!

Make laundry more fun by turning on some tunes, reading a book, or playing a game while you're waiting for a load to finish.

DAY 25

# ON THE TEAM

"I chose you."

—JOHN 15:16 NCV

There's one thing that is no fun at all: being chosen last. I should know. After all, it happens to me *a lot*! I'm just not that athletic. I'd much rather curl up with a book or spend the afternoon painting than play volleyball or kickball or . . . well . . . pretty much any kind of ball. But sooner or later, the day comes in PE class when the two captains choose who will play on their teams. And no one wants me.

I'll be honest, that really used to bother me. But not so much anymore. That's because one night I was talking about it to my youth group leader. It had happened again in PE, and I was still a little upset. (If you've ever been picked last, you know how horrible it feels.) That's when my youth group leader explained that God has already chosen me for His team.

There are still times when I'm chosen last, and that's probably never going to be the most fun thing in the world. (Although sometimes Hope is captain, and she picks me first!) But now that I know God has chosen me, I don't mind so much.

If you're usually the last one picked, remember God wants you on His team—first, last, and always. And if you're the one choosing, pick that "last" girl or guy first once in a while. I promise you, you'll make their day!

## A BRAVE GIRL'S PRAYER

Holy Father, thank You for choosing me. I'm always ready to be on Your team. Amen!

Honor

DAY 26

# I CAN DO SOMETHING

"Leave her alone," said Jesus. "Why are you bothering her? She has done a beautiful thing to me. . . . She did what she could."

—MARK 14:6, 8 NIV

After that disaster of trying to fit in with the "cool" kids at school, I started eating lunch with another group. We were all misfits, for lots of different reasons. Some of the reasons were things I couldn't do anything about, except be kind and try to be a friend, of course. But there was one problem some of my new friends had that I could help with.

You see, some of the kids came from families that didn't have a lot of money, and they came to school without supplies. Not only did it hurt their grades, but going to school without what they needed was embarrassing. A pencil might not seem like an important thing, but just wait until you don't have enough money to buy one.

At first I thought I'd just give them the supplies myself. But then I thought that might be awkward. So I talked to our guidance counselor about it, and we decided to set up a kind of free store in a closet in the school office. Next, I worked with my church to collect school supplies. When everything was ready, the principal sent out a message, and soon everyone knew where they could get the supplies they needed. Because kids are going in and out of the office all the time anyway, the people who need the supplies can get them without any embarrassment.

Just like the woman who showered Jesus with perfume before His death (Mark 14:3–9), we're faced with many troubles that we can't fix. But there are things we *can* do. What problem can you do something about so that Jesus can say, "She has done a beautiful thing"?

## A BRAVE GIRL'S PRAYER

Dear God, I know there are some problems I can't do anything about, but there are other things that I can make better. Show me how to help when I can. Amen.

# SCHOOL SUPPLY "STORE"

It's a terrible thing to have to go to school without the supplies you need to succeed. Gather your friends and set up a free "store" with basic supplies to help those in need at your school.

## MATERIALS

computer, printer, and paper for making flyers

boxes or bins for collecting items

bookshelves and tables for displaying items

labels

Pray over your store before you start, as you're sorting and organizing, and each month when you check how things are going. Pray that God will use the store to bring people to Him.

## STEPS

1. Talk to your parents, teacher, and school guidance counselor about your ideas for the store. What ideas do they have?

2. Decide how you will gather supplies and who will help you. Can this be a project for your school, your youth group, or your entire church? Where should people bring their donations?

3. Ask your teacher or guidance counselor where you can set up the store. A library corner, extra classroom, or closet in the office are all good places. You just want kids to be able to get the supplies without being embarrassed.

4. Ask your teacher or guidance counselor for a list of needed supplies, and decide which ones you will gather. Post flyers around your church and neighborhood asking for donations. Be sure to list exactly what's needed and where to bring items. As supplies come in, organize them into boxes or bins—pencils in one box, folders in another, and so on.

5. Set up the store with tables and shelves to display items by category. Bring in the supplies and use labels so it's easy to find everything.

6. Let kids know the supplies are available. You might ask the principal to make an announcement, have your teacher send out an email, or put up flyers in the hall. Be sure to include information about who the store is for.

About once a month, check on your store. Tidy up and make note of any supplies that are running low. Then put out a call for more donations.

If your church is in charge of collecting donations, post a sign in your store saying, "Sponsored by _____ Church."

Hope

# CHEERING UP AND ON

*Let us think of ways to motivate one another to acts of love and good works.*

—HEBREWS 10:24 NLT

When I first started playing baseball, being the only girl was hard. Some people said really hurtful things. A few even booed. But others cheered me on, right from the start, like my parents, my coach, and some of my teammates.

Those cheers kept me going. They gave me the courage to keep getting up to bat, especially after I had struck out. That's when I started to understand how important it is to encourage others.

So when my church friend Avery told me that he was going to be competing in the Special Olympics, I knew exactly what I wanted to do. You see, Avery has Down syndrome, but he's always got a smile for everyone he meets.

Faith, Glory, Gracie, Honor, and I gathered with the rest of the youth group to make signs and banners. Then on the day of the race, we got there early to give Avery plenty of high fives.

Avery was awesome! But the coolest thing was watching the runners who finished first all turn around to cheer on those who were still running. What a wonderful example! Because the fact is, this race called life isn't an easy one to run. And while God is always there for us, it's great to have some people cheering us on too.

If you want an amazing experience of cheering others on, volunteer with your family or youth group at a Special Olympics event. You'll soon find the one who's most encouraged is you!

### A BRAVE GIRL'S PRAYER

Lord, show me who could use cheering up and on today—and please give me just the right words to do it. Amen.

# BEATING THE BLUES

Sing and make music in your hearts to the Lord.

—EPHESIANS 5:19 ICB

_Gracie_

Do you ever have days when you just feel . . . blue? When nothing seems to go your way? Or when, for whatever reason—or no reason at all—you start to feel a little sorry for yourself? I do.

There are days when I still really miss my friends in Pennsylvania. And even though my dad has a good job now, there are some things we can't do because money is still a little tight. Then there are times when nothing is really wrong, but I just don't feel right.

So yeah, I feel blue sometimes. And that's totally normal. But I don't want to let the blues beat me. So whenever I'm feeling down, I use a good beat to beat the blues. I know, I know! It sounds so corny, but trust me on this. I go into my room, close the door, and turn on my playlist of praise songs—the ones with the super-happy beat. I turn them up really loud. No, I mean _REALLY LOUD_! I grab my hairbrush (also known as my microphone), and I dance and sing all around my room. (Sometimes my mom hears and comes to join me, which is really funny!)

I know this might seem a little silly at first, but it works for me. Try making your own "Beat the Blues" playlist . . . because there's nothing like a happy beat to put a little happiness back in your heart.

## A BRAVE GIRL'S PRAYER

Lord, when I'm feeling blue, remind me of all the reasons You give me to smile. Amen.

Glory

# A BEAUTIFUL CORNER

The LORD God put the man in the garden of
Eden to care for it and work it.

—GENESIS 2:15 NCV

Do you know what the very first job God gave to Adam and Eve was? To take care of the earth—and it's a job He still wants us to do today.

Now, I know that if you look at my polished nails and fancy boots, you might not guess that I'm really passionate about taking care of the earth. That probably sounds more like Hope, who lives on a farm, or Honor, with her love of all things science. The truth is that I adore beautiful things, and the earth is one of the most beautiful things of all. That's why I want to do whatever I can to help keep it as gorgeous as it can be.

Around the house I help my mom take care of the recycling by rinsing out jars, collecting paper, and making sure the recycling bins get taken to the curb on the right day. At school I talked our principal into putting recycling bins for plastic bottles in the lunchroom. And about once a month the Brave Girls head out with our youth group to pick up trash around our church's neighborhood.

Maybe you think keeping the earth beautiful is too big a job for you and your friends. But you don't have to keep the *whole* earth beautiful; just focus on your corner of it.
Try this: Gather a group of friends to help clean up the stands after a
school game. See who can collect the most plastic bottles. And
maybe treat the winner to ice cream!

### A BRAVE GIRL'S PRAYER

Lord, thank You for this beautiful
earth. Help me do my part to keep it
as nice as You made it to be. Amen.

Recycle

# GeT CReaTive

In the beginning God created the heavens and the earth.

—GENESIS 1:1 NIV

Have you ever thought about how creative God is? I mean, just look at this world He made. And since we're all made in His image, that means we're all creative too!

Maybe you draw, paint, sculpt, dance, or sing. Or maybe you don't. You might even be thinking, *Faith, I'm not even a little bit creative.* The fact is, you don't have to be "artistic" to be creative.

Maybe you're fabulous at turning a room full of junk into an organized space. Or perhaps you're great at whipping up a homemade snack without ever glancing at a recipe. Or maybe you creatively solve problems like Honor. (You should see her last science project. How does she even think like that?)

Painting is the way I express my creativity. When I'm painting, I connect with God on a whole different level. I guess that's because, in a very small way, I'm creating just like He creates. There's one painting technique I especially love—and absolutely anyone can do it. Seriously, if you can pour liquid out of a cup, you can create your own masterpiece. Just check out the next page, and I'll show you how.

No matter how you express your creativity, it's definitely there inside you—because your Creator put it there. So let it out! Get out and get creative today.

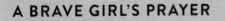

## A BRAVE GIRL'S PRAYER

Holy Father, show me how I can creatively praise You today! Amen.

# POURING TO PAINT

You won't believe the masterpiece that this oh-so-simple style of painting will make!

TIME: 30 MINUTES, PLUS DRYING

## MATERIALS

1 large plastic garbage bag

4 metal food cans

8 x 10-inch (20 x 30-cm) canvas

5 disposable cups

4-ounce bottle of Elmer's Glue-All (Elmer's school glue will not work)

water

5 wooden craft sticks

5 colors of acrylic craft paint

disposable gloves

toothpicks

## TOOLS

measuring spoons

## STEPS

1. Cover your work area with a large plastic garbage bag to catch paint drips.

2. Place the 4 food cans on top of the garbage bag. Set your canvas on top of the cans. (This will keep your canvas from sticking to the garbage bag.)

3. Pour 2 teaspoons (10 ml) of glue and ¹/₂ teaspoon (3 ml) of water into each of the 5 cups. Put a wooden craft stick in each cup and use it to mix the glue and water.

4. Add 2 teaspoons (10 ml) of paint to each cup. Each color should go in a separate cup.

5. Use the wooden craft sticks to mix each color thoroughly. Pop any bubbles. Throw away the sticks.

6. Put on the gloves, and begin pouring the colors onto the canvas in wavy lines, strips, dots—whatever you like. Add the paints in any order. Pour out almost all your paint, but save a little bit of each color in case you need to fill in a blank spot.

7. Gently tilt the canvas from side to side to spread the paint across the entire surface. Use the saved paint to fill in any holes, if necessary. If bubbles appear, use a toothpick to carefully pop them.

8. Allow your canvas to dry. It may take 1 to 3 days to dry completely.

Gracie

# JUST HANG OUT

You will teach me how to live a holy life.
Being with you will fill me with joy.

—PSALM 16:11 NCV

Is there someone you love to be around simply because they make you happy? Maybe it's your mom or dad, or your best friend. For me, it's the Brave Girls.

You see, when I first moved to this town, I didn't know anyone. I didn't really even know about God. Hope, Glory, Honor, and Faith not only reached out to me and became my friends, they also helped me learn about the Lord. (By the way, those are the best kinds of friends—the ones who help us get closer to God.) Being around the Brave Girls fills me up with happiness and joy.

And so does being with God. Did you know that you can just hang out with Him? And that He really wants to hang out with you? That's something the Brave Girls taught me—God *wants* to be with us. We don't have to be praying or praising; we can just be still with Him, or be busy with Him by our side. Imagine . . . *God*, the One who created this whole world, wants to spend the whole day with us! Knowing that fills me with joy deep down inside my heart. And when I think about it, I can't help but smile!

There's a verse in Hebrews that's become special to me: "Feel free to come before God's throne" (4:16 ICB). Be sure to do that—spend time with God today.

## A BRAVE GIRL'S PRAYER

Holy Father, I am so grateful that You want to spend time with me. Thank You! Amen.

# PHONY FUN

The orders of the Lord are right; they make people happy. The commands of the Lord are pure; they light up the way.

—PSALM 19:8 NCV

Have you ever fallen for phony fun? You know, the stuff that people *say* is fun—and that may even look fun at first—but ends up being no fun at all. Stuff like gossiping, cheating, and shoplifting. There are even kids at my school who've tried alcohol and drugs! They lie to their parents to sneak out to parties. They say it's fun, but I see all the trouble it causes—and that doesn't look fun to me at all.

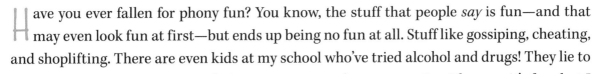

I'll admit, though, when I started at this new school, I wanted to fit in so badly that I did some things I'm not proud of. Like when the "cool" girls invited me to sit with them at lunch. They seemed to have so much fun spreading rumors and gossiping that I tried it too. Then when I was *un*invited from the "cool" table, I saw how hurtful those things they (and I) said could be.

I've thought about it, and I believe God gives us rules—like don't gossip—for a reason: He knows we'll be much happier if we avoid that kind of phony fun. God's rules set us free from worrying about what to do or not do. And if we've already decided to follow what He says, it's easier to choose what's right when we're faced with phony fun.

Make a list of the phony fun things other people do, and decide now what God wants you to do when those things come up in your life.

## A BRAVE GIRL'S PRAYER

Lord, help me say no to the temptations of phony fun. Amen.

DAY 33

# FRIENDS WHO PRAY

I pray that the God who gives hope will fill you with much joy and peace while you trust in Him.

—ROMANS 15:13 NCV

Have you ever heard that saying, "Families who pray together stay together"? Well, the Brave Girls switched that up to "*Friends* who pray together stay together." Because there's just something wonderful about knowing that your friends are lifting you up to God and asking Him to work in your life. And it feels just as great to do the same thing for them.

You see, even though each of us is really blessed, we've also had to deal with some tough stuff lately. Stuff like Glory's parents divorcing and like Honor forgetting that she is God's girl. There were some big problems in our lives, much too big for us to handle on our own. So we decided to pray for each other every day.

Because we all go to different schools, we set up a group chat on our phones so that we could text each other any special prayer requests—and praises for answered prayers, of course! We also try to meet for a few minutes before or after youth group to pray together in person. It's pretty amazing to know that when something is troubling me, I can reach out to friends who love me enough to pray for me.

You should try it. Gather your best friends and start praying together today.

**HOPE**
Another reading test today

**GLORY**
Lord, help Hope focus during the test.

**HONOR**
Give her peace and help her do her best.

**HOPE**
Thanks!

## A BRAVE GIRL'S PRAYER

Lord, I lift up my friends to You. Bless and watch over each and every one of them. Amen.

# GROW JOY

The Spirit produces the fruit of love, joy, peace, patience, kindness, goodness, faithfulness, gentleness, self-control.

—GALATIANS 5:22–23 NCV

One of my favorite things about living on the farm is watching things grow. I never get tired of planting a tiny little seed and then watching it become a stalk of corn, a watermelon, or even a huge tree that makes apples, peaches, or pears.

Maybe that's why I love the verses about the fruit of the Spirit. Of course, this isn't the kind of fruit you eat—it's much more amazing than that! The fruit of the Spirit is "planted" when we decide to follow God and the Holy Spirit comes to live inside us. The Spirit "plants" in our hearts the seeds of all the good things that make us more like Jesus—things like being patient and kind, loving and gentle. Just as sunshine and water help plants grow, the fruit of the Spirit grows in the sunshine of prayer and praise and with the water of God's Word.

One of the seeds that the Spirit plants is joy! God gives us reasons to be joyful when the sun is shining and everything is wonderful. He gives us reasons to be joyful when rain and sadness are pouring down—and in every moment in between. The great thing about God's joy is that the more you share it, the bigger it grows. So don't keep it to yourself—share the joy of knowing God with someone today!

## A BRAVE GIRL'S PRAYER

Lord, grow Your joy inside me until it's so big and strong that it just spills out of me and into the world. Amen.

# MINI TERRARIUM

Make your own terrarium—a miniature garden that takes care of itself! Then watch the wonder of the water cycle as the plants soak up the water and release it back into the atmosphere, where it then condenses and "rains" down the sides of the terrarium—ready to begin the cycle all over again.

TIME: 30 MINUTES

## MATERIALS

1 clear glass jar with a tight-fitting lid

small pebbles

activated charcoal or carbon (You can find this wherever fish tank supplies are sold; optional)

potting soil

1 to 2 tiny plants

decorations, such as a small figure, rock, or seashell (optional)

## STEPS

1. Wash your jar and lid with warm, soapy water. Dry completely.

2. Fill the jar about 1 inch (2.5 cm) high with small pebbles.

3. Add half an inch (1.5 cm) of activated charcoal or carbon. This is optional, but it will help the water stay cleaner and your terrarium last longer.

4. Add potting soil until the jar is half full.

5. Use your fingers to dig small holes in the dirt. Gently put your plants in the holes. Cover the roots with dirt, and press the dirt around your plants.

6. Add any decorations.

7. Lightly water and add the lid. Place in a sunny window.

Over the next few weeks, keep an eye on your plants. Add a little more water if the plants dry out. Move it to a sunnier or shadier spot as needed. When you have the right balance of water and light, your terrarium will take care of itself!

Gracie

# A GIFT AND A BLESSING

"I was hungry, and you gave me food."

—MATTHEW 25:35 NCV

There was a time after my dad lost his job that we had a lot of money troubles. There were even a couple of times we didn't have enough money to pay for all our groceries, so Mom had to put some things back. My dad's working again now, and things are much better. But I'll never forget how scared I was watching my mom put back those groceries.

I guess that's why I so love this idea our youth group came up with: a free food pantry. Some of the grown-ups got together and built it. To me, it looks kind of like a giant birdhouse on a stand, except the front opens up and there are shelves inside. It sits in the parking lot of our church where anyone can stop by and take what they need. Our youth group is in charge of making sure it always has food inside—things that won't spoil like peanut butter and cans of soup. We attach a note with a verse or short prayer to each item. And as we put them inside, we pray that the food will fill hungry tummies and the verse will fill hungry hearts.

I can't tell you how good it feels to help make sure someone else doesn't have to worry about food. And every time I put something inside, I remember how blessed I am.

Talk to your youth group or church about creating your own free food pantry or other way to help those in need. Not only will it be a gift to your community, but it will also be a blessing to you.

## A BRAVE GIRL'S PRAYER

Lord, please be with those who are hungry and let them be filled. Amen.

Glory

# Fashion Fun

Encourage each other and build each other up.

—1 THESSALONIANS 5:11 NLT

Posting pictures of new outfits on social media is one of my favorite things to do—at least it was until someone left a comment about how terrible it was to brag about my new stuff. I honestly hadn't thought of it that way. Putting outfits together is something that makes me happy. In fact, someday I plan to design my own line of clothes.

When I talked to my friends about that comment, Gracie admitted that sometimes she felt just a tiny bit bad about herself because her family doesn't have the money to buy a lot of new things. That got me to thinking. I didn't want to give up my fashion styling—it's part of who I am. But what if I could do it in a way that helped others feel better about themselves instead of worse?

I asked Gracie to help me. We went through her closet, and I showed her how to create fresh, new outfits with what she already had. And we had so much fun! We posted pics of her outfits, and a couple of girls at church commented on how much they loved my ideas.

I want everything I do to encourage others, even the stuff I post online. What can you share today—online or in person—to encourage someone? Maybe it's a Bible verse, a stylish outfit, an idea, or simply a smile. Spread some joy!

## A BRAVE GIRL'S PRAYER

Holy Father, show me someone who needs encouraging today. And then help me spread Your joy. Amen.

# LET'S SWAP!

Invite your friends to a clothing swap. Not only is it a great way to clean out your closet, it also lets you do some free shopping and styling with your friends. And those jeans that don't fit your style anymore just might be your best friend's treasure.

TIME: 2 HOURS

## MATERIALS

clothes and accessories to swap

1 floor-length mirror or bathroom wall mirror

1 clothing rack (optional)

cardstock and markers

snacks and drinks

## STEPS

1. Decide on a time and a place for your swap.

2. Invite your friends to bring three or more gently used items to swap. Items can be clothes, shoes, purses, jewelry, and other accessories. Remind them to be sure that nothing is stained or torn. (And don't worry about body sizes. Because you're including accessories and shoes, everyone will be able to find a treasure to take home.)

3. Encourage your friends to dress in clothes that are easy to change in and out of.

4. Before everyone arrives, set up your swap area. Place the mirror in an area set aside for trying on clothes. (Or just use a bathroom with a large mirror as the fitting room.) Hang large items on the rack, if you have one. Use the cardstock and markers to create labels and place them around the room to organize the items.

5. Set up a snack area away from the clothes—just in case!

6. As everyone arrives, sort items into the appropriate areas. Let everyone "window-shop" for the first few minutes to see what's available.

7. Next, it's time to let everyone shop. Take turns or draw numbers, but make sure everyone gets a chance. Continue taking turns until all the wanted items are claimed.

8. Gather any unwanted items and donate them to charity. (Talk to your school's guidance counselor. They often keep a "closet" for kids who need something to wear.)

DAY 37

# BRIGHTEN SOMEONE'S DAY

[Jesus] came to a certain village where a woman named Martha welcomed Him into her home.

—LUKE 10:38 NLT

In our Bible class the other day, we were talking about Mary and Martha. You know, the two sisters who were friends of Jesus. Mary gets a lot of praise—and rightly so—for listening to Jesus teach instead of worrying about dinner (Luke 10:38–42). But I think Martha would be a good person to have around too. After all, there are *plenty* of times when we need someone to step up and take care of others.

Our youth group does this by visiting nursing homes. We each use our own talents to try to brighten the residents' day. Gracie likes to lead a sing-along, and Glory gives manicures. Hope and Honor usually gather a group to play cards and checkers. But my favorite thing to do is ask a nurse which residents don't get any visitors. Those are the people I focus on. Mostly I just ask a question or two. Then once they start telling their stories, I listen—they tell the most amazing stories! I might ask questions like these: What kinds of things did you do after school when you were my age? What was your favorite subject in school? What's the biggest change or the craziest invention you've seen?

Ask your parents or youth group about visiting a nursing home or someone else who has a hard time getting out of the house. You'll learn a lot—and you'll find that brightening their day brightens yours too!

### A BRAVE GIRL'S PRAYER

Lord, teach me how to reach out to the older people around me. Amen.

# SHINE!

"In the same way, you should be a light for other people. Live so that they will see the good things you do and will praise your Father in heaven."

—MATTHEW 5:16 NCV

Honor

I love experiments and inventing things. To me, there's nothing more amazing than discovering how to make things happen. So when I read about using a potato as a power source to light a lightbulb, I just knew I had to try it.

Well, I worked my way step-by-step through the "invention," and guess what? It worked! Now, it's not the brightest light in the world, so I took it inside a dark room to test it out. And that little light lit up the whole room!

It reminded me of that song we sing with the little kids at church sometimes. You've probably heard it too. It's the one about letting our lights shine. Sometimes it seems like there's so much darkness in this world. Not the turn-the-light-off kind of darkness, but the darkness of actual evil and the terrible things that happen. It makes me wonder if the good things I try to do make any difference at all. But that little potato light reminded me of just how powerful light—God's light—is. And when we shine it into the world, it chases the darkness away.

Ask God to help you shine the light of His love into your world today. Be kind and helpful. Share and smile. Sing and praise. Talk to someone about Him. Because even a little light can chase away a lot of darkness.

## A BRAVE GIRL'S PRAYER

Lord, thank You for the light of Your love that You shine into my life. Teach me to shine into the world around me. Amen.

# SHINE YOUR . . . POTATO LIGHT?

Yes! You can actually use a potato to power a lightbulb. Okay, it's a really tiny lightbulb—but still, isn't the science of God's creation amazing?

TIME: 20 MINUTES

## MATERIALS

2 large potatoes

4 shiny pennies

5 pieces of copper wire, each about 12 inches (30 cm) long

4 zinc-plated (or galvanized) nails

1 small lightbulb

## TOOLS

knife (use with a grown-up's help)

wire cutters

## STEPS

1. With an adult's help, cut the potatoes in half longways.

2. Cut a small slit on one side of each half, big enough to put a penny in.

3. Wrap a piece of copper wire around each penny three or four times. Push the pennies at least halfway into the slits in each potato. There should be a "tail" of wire sticking out from each penny.

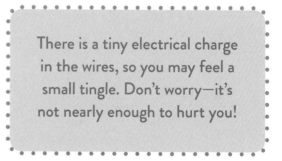

There is a tiny electrical charge in the wires, so you may feel a small tingle. Don't worry—it's not nearly enough to hurt you!

72

4. Insert a nail into three of the potato halves. Make sure the nails don't touch the pennies.

5. In the potato halves with the nails, take the wires connected to three of the pennies and wrap them around the nail in the neighboring potato (your potatoes will form a semicircle). Wrap wire tightly around the last nail and insert it into the remaining potato half.

6. Twist the two loose wires around the metal base of the lightbulb and watch it light up. (It's a small light, so you may need to turn out the lights to see it.)

Hope

1

# A MASTERPIECE IN THE MAKING

*God began doing a good work in you, and I am sure He will continue it until it is finished when Jesus Christ comes again.*

—PHILIPPIANS 1:6 NCV

I blew it. I *really* blew it. You see, my friends and I worked all afternoon on a special cake for a youth group party. We baked and frosted and decorated. It was a masterpiece! But then . . . I tripped over a toy one of my brothers had left lying around and fell face-first into the cake. At first everyone was shocked, but then they started to giggle. Everyone except me, that is. I was so embarrassed. I had ruined everything! I completely lost my temper and yelled at my brothers. Then I stomped off to my room and hid under the covers for a big, long cry.

It wasn't long before my mom came to find me. I thought she'd be mad, but she just pulled me in close for a hug. "Nobody's perfect," she said. "Everyone makes mistakes and loses their cool. God's still working on you. In fact, you're His masterpiece in the making. It's what you do *next* that matters most."

So I dried my tears and apologized to my friends and my brothers. Then we took the cake—the part that didn't have my faceprint in it—and scooped it into cupcake liners. *Presto!* Deconstructed cake! (Turns out it's a really "in" thing!)

The next time you mess up (and we all do!), remember that no one is perfect and that God is still working on you!

## A BRAVE GIRL'S PRAYER

Lord, I want to be the masterpiece You created me to be. Thank You for always working on me and for not giving up on me when I make a mistake. Amen.

Glory

DAY 40

# WHAT'S YOUR "THING"?

Each of you has received a gift to use to serve others.

—1 PETER 4:10 NCV

We've all got our "thing"—something God made us especially good at. For Hope, it's sports, and for Honor, it's books and learning. Faith is an amazing artist, while Gracie sings like an angel. It's so obvious what my friends are good at that, honestly, I was starting to feel a bit bad. I love fashion and beautiful things, but how can I use that to serve God?

Then in school we learned about this thing called *brainstorming*. It's when you think about a topic and then write down whatever pops into your head. So I grabbed some colorful paper and a glitter pen. (I mentioned that I like pretty things, right?) I said a quick prayer for God to guide my thinking and then I asked myself, *What can I do with this love of beauty God has given me?* It took a few minutes of thinking, but then all kinds of ideas came to me! I can use fashion to help others feel better about themselves. I can collect clothes for those in need. I can teach others to see the beauty all around them. And on and on—the ideas just kept coming!

What do you love to do? What are you really great at? Those things are gifts from God. He put that love and that ability in you for a reason. How can you use your gift for good—and for God—today?

## A BRAVE GIRL'S PRAYER

Lord, help me see the gifts You've given me, and then teach me to use them for You. Amen.

# I ♥ BEING ME! BOARD

Fill a bulletin board with words and pictures of the things you love, the things that inspire you, and the things you dream of doing someday.

**TIME: 2 HOURS**

## MATERIALS

pretty paper

colored pens

photos and pictures cut from magazines or printed off the internet

1 cork bulletin board, any size

thumbtacks

## TOOLS

scissors

## STEPS

1. Write three lists, each one on a different kind of paper:

   - My Talents

   - What Makes Me Smile

   - My Dreams

2. Find photos, pictures from magazines, or pictures printed from the internet (with a parent's permission) that represent your list.

3. On other pieces of paper, write or print words, verses, or sayings that make you feel good about yourself and inspire you to reach your dreams. Cut out each item so it's on its own piece of paper.

4. Arrange your lists, words, and images on the bulletin board to create an artful display. Use thumbtacks to hold everything in place. Add to your board anytime you find a word or picture that inspires you. Revisit it every few weeks to see if there are things you want to change.

5. Hang your bulletin board wherever you can see it often and be inspired!

DAY 41

# SEEING THE INVISIBLE

Happy are those who think about the poor.

—PSALM 41:1 NCV

Did you know there are invisible people in this world? No, not the I-can-see-right-through-them kind of invisible. These are the people we seem to *choose* not to see. They're the ones holding up signs, asking for money on the street corners. They're the homeless you see sleeping on benches and in the alleys. If you live in a big city, you've probably seen a lot of these people—*if*, that is, you choose to really see them.

Our youth group leader says that we sometimes pretend not to see homeless people because they make us uncomfortable. But he reminded us that each of them is someone Jesus sees and loves and died to save. So we should see and love and help them too. The question is . . . how?

The Brave Girls put our heads together and came up with this idea: We take a pair of new socks and stuff one inside the other, along with a water bottle and a granola bar. If it's cold outside, we add a hand warmer or two. Then we write out a prayer and add a Bible verse to tuck inside. We also make cards that say "We're here to help" with our church's phone number and address. We keep these "kits" in our parents' cars to hand out to people in need (with our parents' permission, of course). We can't fix their lives, but we can *see* them, pray for them, and brighten their day. And that makes me—and God—happy!

Is there someone you can "see" and love and help today?

### A BRAVE GIRL'S PRAYER

Lord, teach me to see the people around me who are hurting and in need. And give me the wisdom to know how I can help. Amen.

*Honor*

# SWEETER THAN HONEY

YOUR PROMISES ARE SWEET TO ME, SWEETER THAN HONEY IN MY MOUTH!
—PSALM 119:103 NCV

Let's face it, in this crazy world it's easy to forget who you are and *whose* you are. I know because it wasn't that long ago when *I* was struggling to remember that I was God's girl. That's when the Brave Girls came together to encourage me and remind me of God's promises. They each gave me their favorite verses, and together, we memorized them all.

These days I *know* I'm God's girl—even though I'm not perfect at it. But there are still times when it's great to have a reminder. That's when I pull up one of God's promises in my mind and hold it close to my heart. His words really are sweet, and they give me the courage to keep going.

I'll bet there are days you could use a reminder of God's promises too. Here are some of my faves:

- "For I know the plans I have for you," declares the LORD, "plans to prosper you and not to harm you, plans to give you hope and a future." (Jeremiah 29:11 NIV)

- "Be strong and courageous. Do not be afraid; do not be discouraged, for the LORD your God will be with you wherever you go." (Joshua 1:9 NIV)

- Trust the LORD with all your heart, and don't depend on your own understanding. Remember the LORD in all you do, and He will give you success. (Proverbs 3:5-6 NCV)

Get with your friends and memorize your favorite Bible promises. Plan to learn a new verse each week. It'll be so much easier—and more fun—together.

## A BRAVE GIRL'S PRAYER

Dear God, thank You for Your sweet promises. I know You'll keep every single one! Amen.

# EASY PEANUT BUTTER FUDGE

Make this sweet treat to enjoy with your friends while you
work to memorize the sweet promises of God.

TIME: 1 HOUR AND 15 MINUTES

MAKES: 36 LARGE PIECES

## INGREDIENTS

½ cup (113 g) butter, cut in chunks

1 cup (175 g) semisweet chocolate chips

1 bag (10 oz; 280 g) peanut butter chips

14 ounces (396 ml) sweetened condensed milk

## TOOLS

9 x 9-inch (23 x 23-cm) pan

waxed paper

microwave-safe bowl

silicone spatula

microwave

cutting board

butter knife

## STEPS

1. Line a 9 x 9-inch pan with waxed paper.

2. Place all ingredients in a microwave-safe bowl and stir.

3. Microwave for 4 minutes on the low or defrost setting.

4. Use the spatula to stir until smooth.

5. Pour into the lined 9 x 9-inch pan.

6. Chill in the refrigerator for 1 hour, or until firm.

7. Pull up on the wax paper to loosen the fudge. Then flip the pan upside down on a cutting board. Gently tug on the wax paper until the fudge falls out. Peel off the waxed paper, and slice into squares.

Gracie

# LIGHTS, CAMERA . . .
# MOVIE TIME!

Be ready to welcome guests.

—TITUS 1:8 NCV

So here's the thing . . . when I first became part of the Brave Girls, I wanted to invite them over to hang out at my house. But I didn't because I was a little worried that my house wasn't good enough. You see, Glory has this great beach house we go to sometimes, Honor has all these interesting pets to play with, Hope lives on a farm (complete with baby cows and chicks), and Faith has this amazing art studio. Don't get me wrong; my house is great, but it's just a, well, *house*. No beach, no interesting pets, no baby animals, and no art studio. Plus, we don't have a lot of money right now to spend on entertaining.

When my mom asked me why I hadn't invited my friends over, I broke down and told her. That's when she reminded me that friendship isn't about what you do or where you go; it's about being together. Then she suggested we do a movie night. We could borrow a movie from the library and pop some popcorn. So that's just what we did. We found a great Christian film that helped us learn more about God even while we were laughing and crying together. It was so much fun—and it cost hardly a thing. That night I realized that true friends don't care about where you live or what you can give them. They love you just because you're you.

Gather up your true friends for a movie night—and don't forget the popcorn!

### A BRAVE GIRL'S PRAYER

Lord, teach me to open my home and my heart to others. Amen.

DAY 44

# RAKE AND RUN

We are God's workers, working together.
—1 CORINTHIANS 3:9 NCV

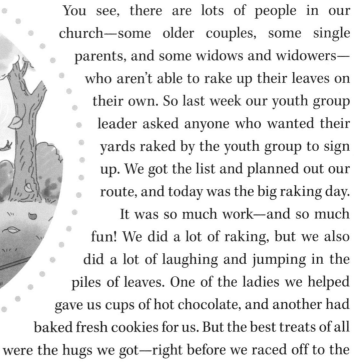

Whew! I'm exhausted. Today I went with the Brave Girls and the rest of the youth group on a service project. We called it "Rake and Run." Basically, we went around to a bunch of different yards, raked up leaves as fast as we could, and then ran to the next yard.

You see, there are lots of people in our church—some older couples, some single parents, and some widows and widowers—who aren't able to rake up their leaves on their own. So last week our youth group leader asked anyone who wanted their yards raked by the youth group to sign up. We got the list and planned out our route, and today was the big raking day.

It was so much work—and so much fun! We did a lot of raking, but we also did a lot of laughing and jumping in the piles of leaves. One of the ladies we helped gave us cups of hot chocolate, and another had baked fresh cookies for us. But the best treats of all were the hugs we got—right before we raced off to the next yard.

If your friends, family, or youth group is looking for a simple and inexpensive way to help others, try your own "Rake and Run." It's so much fun!

## A BRAVE GIRL'S PRAYER

Lord, show me creative ways to help others—and to have fun! Amen.

Glory

# HOW BEAUTIFUL!

The twelve gates were twelve pearls, each gate having been made from a single pearl. And the street of the city was made of pure gold as clear as glass.

—REVELATION 21:21 NCV

Have you ever read what the Bible says heaven will look like? It sounds amazing! Gates made from a single pearl, streets of pure gold, a wall of jasper. (Yeah, I had to look that one up too. Turns out jasper is this multicolored gemstone that comes in colors from reddish-brown and yellow to even green and blue.)

Our lives in heaven will be beautiful too. God promises there will be no more sickness or sadness (Revelation 21:4). There won't be any darkness either because it will be lit up day and night with the glory of God (Revelation 22:5).

There's even a verse in 1 Corinthians that says, "No eye has seen, no ear has heard, and no mind has imagined what God has prepared for those who love him" (2:9 NLT). We can't even imagine how beautiful heaven will be!

Sometimes when I see something truly amazing in God's creation, I stop and think to myself, *God made this so beautiful, but heaven will be a million times better!* The next time you see something that just makes you stop and say, "Wow!" remember that heaven will be even more wonderful—and that God made it for you!

### A BRAVE GIRL'S PRAYER

Lord, I praise You for all the beauty You have given us in this world—it's amazing to think heaven will be even more wonderful! Amen.

Faith

# IN BUSINESS

Lord our God, be pleased with us. Give us success in what we do.
—PSALM 90:17 ICB

When school was *finally* out for summer, my friends and I wanted to do something special together. We decided we'd all love to spend the day at an amusement park. The thing is, those parks are expensive. My parents said they would take everyone, but we had to pay for our own tickets. And since none of us had that much money saved up, we decided to set up our own babysitting business to earn it.

It was hard work, and we learned plenty of dos and don'ts along the way. (Check out our best tips coming up next.) All summer long, we saved. I'll admit there were times when it was hard to have money jingling in our pockets and not spend it. But Honor helped us come up with a budget to keep us on track. Every week we made sure to give some back to God—after all, He gives us *everything*! And there were even a couple times we gave extra, like when the church was raising money to buy Bibles to send overseas and when the college kids were fundraising to dig wells for people to have clean water. Even though it meant saving up for our tickets would take a little longer, it felt really great to be able to give our own money to help.

By the end of the summer, we had earned all the money we needed. And the amusement park was awesome! Also, I think we actually enjoyed it more because we earned it!

## A BRAVE GIRL'S PRAYER

God, I thank You for the ability to work. Please always bless me with work I love to do. Amen.

# THE BUSINESS OF BABYSITTING

Starting your own babysitting business is a great way to make money and a wonderful way to serve your community. Babysit on your own or coordinate with friends to take on more jobs.

## STEPS

1. Find out how to babysit. Ask older friends or siblings about their experiences. Check out babysitting books from the library. Also consider taking a babysitting course to become certified. These courses are often offered by the Red Cross at a community center and include first aid and CPR. Being trained will show your babysitting clients that you have the skills to keep their children safe.

2. Think about who you will babysit. They might be younger cousins or kids from your church or neighborhood. Be sure to get your parents' approval for any new clients.

3. Decide how much you will charge per hour. Babysitters usually earn somewhere between $5 and $15 an hour. Ask other babysitters how much they charge. Do they charge extra for multiple kids? Or for things like helping with homework?

4. Create a simple flyer to hand out to possible clients. Include your name, phone number, and the days you're usually available. Add two to three references from people who will vouch for how responsible you are. As a bonus, add a list of what activities you can do with the kids, such as prepare snacks, do crafts, help with homework, play games, and read stories.

5. Before sitting for a new client, visit them for an interview. Meet the children and find out what the parents expect of you. Take notes about family rules, allergies, and

> Consider donating your babysitting services to a single parent or to someone who can't usually afford a babysitter.

emergency phone numbers. (And if you feel uncomfortable for any reason, it's okay to say no.)

6. Use a planner or a calendar to keep track of your jobs. If you're working with a group of friends, set up a way, like a group text or shared calendar, to keep each other informed of jobs.

## Emergency Tips

- Learn basic first aid.
- Get the parents' phone numbers in case of emergency.
- Know the address—just in case you have to call 9-1-1.

## Babysitting Tips

- Plan plenty of activities, such as art projects, games, or a movie with popcorn. Don't spend the whole time watching TV though. And if you're going to go outside or to a park, check with the parents first.
- Always tidy up after activities. Parents don't want to come back to a mess!
- Create a Fun Bag to take with you. Toss in storybooks, coloring books, and crayons, along with a few simple toys. Seeing something new is often enough to distract a cranky child.

Gracie

DAY 47

# J.O.Y.

"Love the Lord your God with all your heart, all your soul, and all your mind." . . . "Love your neighbor as you love yourself."

—MATTHEW 22:37, 39 NCV

Have you heard of the J.O.Y. principle? My youth leader told us about it a little while ago, and it's been a joy (ha!) to use it in my life. You see, each of the letters stands for something: J for *Jesus*, O for *others*, and Y for *you*. J.O.Y. tells us how we should live our lives—loving Jesus first, others second, and ourselves last.

When I first learned about the J.O.Y. principle, I decided to try to live it out. So every day I do something that shows Jesus how much I love Him. It might be singing a praise song, praying, or learning something about Him. I also try to show someone else how much I love them. Some days it might be a big thing, like helping out at the homeless shelter or babysitting for free. Other days it's something small, like helping my mom do the dishes, texting something encouraging to a friend, or simply telling my dad I love him. And lastly, I try to do something loving for myself—like taking time to do something I love or making sure I say only kind things to myself.

J.O.Y. adds so much . . . well . . . *joy* to my life. Challenge yourself to put some J.O.Y. in your day today—and every day. You won't believe the difference it makes!

## A BRAVE GIRL'S PRAYER

Lord, teach me to live by the J.O.Y. principle— and fill my life with You and Your joy. Amen.

Glory

DAY 48

# GIVE A LITTLE GRACE

Thanks be to God for His gift that is too wonderful for words.
—2 CORINTHIANS 9:15 NCV

Have you ever been given a gift that is just too wonderful for words? Maybe it was a birthday gift or a Christmas gift. Once, my mom gave me a trip to the beach with all the Brave Girls. *That* was pretty much too wonderful for words. But if you've decided to follow Jesus, then you already have a gift more wonderful than anything that would fit under a tree or in a box, or even in a whole beach house! You have the gift of God's grace. And *that* is a reason to live brave with lots of joy.

Think about it this way: grace means that when you mess up and sin—whether it was by accident or on purpose—God will forgive you. You don't have to carry around a load of guilt, and you don't have to be separated from God (because that's what sin does).

Here's the curious thing though: when you *give* away that same grace to others, it brings still more joy to your life. That's because *everybody* makes mistakes. There will be a day when even your best friend messes up, says the wrong thing, or hurts your feelings. If you will give her the same kind of grace God gives to you, then you can get back to being friends and having fun together. So give a little grace today . . . because God has given so much grace to you.

## A BRAVE GIRL'S PRAYER

Holy Father, when I'm feeling hurt or wronged, help me give a little grace. And thank You for giving me so much. Amen.

89

Honor

DAY 49

# SMILE!

Happiness makes a person smile.

—PROVERBS 15:13 NCV

Have you ever heard the saying that a smile is just a frown turned upside down? Yeah, it's a little cheesy. But as it turns out, there's some truth in that old saying. Smiling can actually change your mood and help you feel happier. Scientists aren't really sure why, but *I* think maybe it's because smiling reminds your face of what it's like to feel happy—and all the things there are to be happy about.

We really do have so many things to smile about, and each and every one of them is a blessing from God. Plus, He *loves* to see His children smile. Make it your goal to find something to smile about today and every day. No matter how tough things are, God is always there to give you something good.

There's another interesting fact about smiles you should know: they're contagious! Yep, they spread like the flu—except they're much nicer to catch! Set up your own smile experiment and test it out. As you go through your day today, smile at the people you meet and keep track of how many smile back. See how many smiles you can gather in one day. You could even challenge your friends to join in and see who can collect the most smiles.

### A BRAVE GIRL'S PRAYER

Lord, thank You for giving me so many reasons to smile. Remind me to let my joy show on my face. Amen.

# SWEET SURPRISE

Every time I think of you, I give thanks to my God.
—PHILIPPIANS 1:3 NLT

Hope

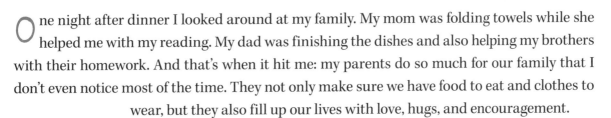

One night after dinner I looked around at my family. My mom was folding towels while she helped me with my reading. My dad was finishing the dishes and also helping my brothers with their homework. And that's when it hit me: my parents do so much for our family that I don't even notice most of the time. They not only make sure we have food to eat and clothes to wear, but they also fill up our lives with love, hugs, and encouragement.

Like my dad. He's my biggest cheerleader and goes to practically every one of my games. Sometimes he even makes a sign to wave around when I come up to bat. It's kind of embarrassing, but secretly . . . I love it!

And my mom is so great about helping me with my reading. This dyslexia thing makes me stumble over the same word again and again, but she never gets frustrated. She just encourages me to keep trying.

I decided to do something special for my parents to say thank you. And I knew just the right thing. The next Saturday I got up early and made homemade muffins, just the way my mom taught me. (Her recipe is on the next page.) I put them on a tray with glasses of milk and juice and added a flower from our garden to make it pretty. Then I tiptoed in . . . and they loved my surprise!

Whether it's your parents, your grandparents, a special neighbor, a teacher, or a friend, how can you surprise someone who does so much for you?

## A BRAVE GIRL'S PRAYER

Lord, thank You for all the people in my life who take such good care of me. Amen.

# MIX-IN MUFFINS

This recipe makes a wonderfully sweet bread that you can use as a base for any kind of muffin. Choose chocolate chips, blueberries, or any other baking chip, fruit, or nut.

TIME: 30 MINUTES

MAKES: 12 MUFFINS

## INGREDIENTS

2 cups (240 g) all-purpose flour

$^2/_3$ cup (130 g) sugar

1 tablespoon (15 g) baking powder

$^1/_4$ teaspoon (1.5 g) salt

1 large egg

$^2/_3$ cup (160 ml) milk

1 teaspoon (5 ml) vanilla extract

$^1/_2$ cup (113 g) melted butter, cooled

2 cups (300 g) mix-ins: chocolate chips or blueberries or something else!

## TOOLS

12-cup muffin tin

12 muffin liners

2 mixing bowls

measuring cups and spoons

whisk

silicone spatula

oven (ask an adult for help)

## STEPS

1. Preheat the oven to 425 degrees Fahrenheit (218 degrees C).

2. Place muffin liners in the muffin tin.

3. In a large mixing bowl, add the flour, sugar, baking powder, and salt. Whisk until well mixed.

4. In a separate bowl, add the egg, milk, vanilla, and melted butter. Whisk until well mixed.

5. Pour the wet mixture into the dry mixture. Stir with a spatula until just combined. The batter should still be lumpy.

6. Add your mix-in (chocolate chips, blueberries, or something else).

7. Pour the batter into the muffin cups. Fill each cup about two-thirds full.

8. Bake for 10 minutes. Then turn the oven down to 350 degrees Fahrenheit (177 degrees C) and bake for 5 more minutes—or until a toothpick stuck in the middle of a muffin comes out with only a few moist crumbs on it.

Faith

DAY 51

# SERVING THOSE WHO SERVE

*"I am with you and will protect you everywhere you go."*

—GENESIS 28:15 NCV

A few months ago, our church threw a huge going-away party for one of our members—she was a soldier heading off to war. I was so proud of her courage! But as I watched her hugging everyone goodbye, I thought about how lonely it must be to go so far away from your home and your family—and how scary it would be to go to a place where there is so much danger. And she was going to be gone for *so* long. The Brave Girls and I decided that we would make sure she knew she was loved and remembered.

At least once a month, we put together a care package for her. Inside it, we put things like cards and letters, gum, books, and magazines. And I always paint her a picture of home. At Christmas, we even sent her a small tree with twinkle lights!

Chances are you have some soldiers in your church or neighborhood who could use a letter or even a care package from home. (Your parents can help you search the internet for ideas of what to send and not send.) If you don't know any soldiers, check out the website OperationGratitude.com for ways to send letters and gifts to soldiers. Our troops do so much for us—it's great to be able to do something special for them!

## A BRAVE GIRL'S PRAYER

Lord, please watch over all those in harm's way and bring them safely home. Amen.

DAY 52

# BUILDERS

Let everything you say be good and helpful, so that your words will be an encouragement to those who hear them.

—EPHESIANS 4:29 NLT

One of the first things I learned when my family started going to church is how God created everything just by speaking. That's so incredible to me! It's hard to even imagine that kind of power. God spoke and things—*big things*—happened. Stars soared into the sky and animals roared to life.

I'm starting to realize that God gave us a little bit of that same power. It's true! When we speak, things happen. Okay, so our words aren't going to raise any mountains into the sky or carve out any canyons, but we can do some serious building up or—if we're not careful—tearing down.

Our words are powerful things. And sadly, some people think it's fun to gossip, spread lies and rumors, and tear others down with their words. Chances are you probably know how horrible it feels to be on the receiving end of that kind of "fun." What *is* fun is watching someone bloom right in front of you when you lift them up with praise and encouragement.

Before you speak today—and every day—ask yourself what you're about to create with your words. Make sure it's something that would make God smile!

## A BRAVE GIRL'S PRAYER

Lord, help me be careful with the words I say. Amen.

95

# BEaUTiFUL WORDS COLLaGe

Turn your favorite verse or saying into a work of art!

TIME: 1 HOUR, PLUS DRYING TIME

## MATERIALS

1 favorite verse or saying

scrapbook paper, magazines, and photos

pencil

1 blank canvas of any size

dark-colored permanent marker

watercolor paints

Mod Podge

## TOOLS

scissors

foam brush

## STEPS

1. Decide on the theme for your collage. It could be flowers, water, or your favorite color.

2. Choose a saying or verse.

3. Pick out scrapbook paper, magazine pictures, and photos that fit your theme. Cut them into wavy strips or other shapes. Cut out enough to completely cover your canvas.

4. Use a pencil to write your saying or verse on the canvas. Write it any way you would like—in big block letters or fancy script. Leave room for your collage papers.

5. Trace over the pencil lines with permanent marker.

6. Paint your canvas with watercolors and allow to dry.

7. On a table, arrange your pieces just how you want them to appear on the canvas.

8. With the foam brush, paint a thin layer of Mod Podge all over the canvas.

9. Place the collage pieces on the canvas and lightly press down. Brush with more Mod Podge as needed.

10. Let dry 10–15 minutes.

11. To seal your collage, cover the entire canvas with Mod Podge. (Don't worry—it will dry clear!) Let dry overnight. Hang your collage or give it to a friend.

DAY 53

# ONLY HOLY

*A poor widow came and gave two very small copper coins. These coins were not worth even a penny.*

—MARK 12:42 ICB

Because I'm interested in science, I do a lot of measuring. I measure weights, times, distances, and more. That sort of measuring is fun to me. Sometimes, though, I measure myself. And that's not so fun, especially when I measure myself against others.

I look at Hope and know I'll never play ball like her. I look at Faith and know I'll never paint like her. I can't sing like Gracie or see the beauty in everything like Glory. Yeah, I'm good in school and with animals, but sometimes these things feel small compared to what everyone else can do. And that feeling steals my joy.

Then one day I was reading my Bible, and I came across this story about the widow who gave God all she had—even though it was only two tiny copper coins. They weren't even

worth a penny. The amount was *nothing* compared to how much everyone else gave. Yet Jesus said she actually gave *more* than everyone else because it was all she had.

That's when I started thinking that maybe God doesn't measure the same way we do. When it comes to using our gifts to love and serve Him, there's no such thing as big or small. There is only holy. God gave me these gifts of loving animals and science, and He loves when I use them. What gifts has God given you? How can you use them to give back to Him today?

### A BRAVE GIRL'S PRAYER

Lord, I know comparing myself to others is wrong. Thank You for the special gifts You've given me. Teach me to embrace them and use them with joy. Amen.

Art rules

# SUPERHEROES

The LORD has told you . . . what He wants from you: to do what is right to other people, love being kind to others, and live humbly, obeying your God.

—MICAH 6:8 NCV

Sometimes I volunteer to help out in the little kids' Sunday school class. They're just so sweet! And all the kids try to do whatever I do. When I build a tower with blocks, they all start building towers. When I laugh, they giggle. When I say "bless you" because someone sneezes, suddenly there's a whole chorus of "bless you"s all around me.

It's really cute the way they try to copy *whatever* I do. But the other day it hit me: having all these little kids looking up to me is a huge responsibility! I need to make sure I'm being a good example in everything I do and say. It's also a huge joy, though, because "teaching" these little ones is really just playing with them—which is so much fun!

The fact is, we older kids are almost like superheroes to these little kids. We can do things they can't—like read a book by ourselves, tie our own shoes, and make a sandwich. And as "superheroes," we can teach them things, like being kind, sharing, and helping each other, just by playing with them.

Be a superhero and volunteer to help out with the little ones in your church, neighborhood, or even your family. After all, you may not be able to leap tall buildings in a single bound, but you can reach the cookie jar!

## A BRAVE GIRL'S PRAYER

Father, help me be a good example to all the little ones who are looking up to me. Amen.

Hope

DAY 55

# GET OUTSIDE

*"Be still and know that I am God."*

—PSALM 46:10 NCV

With two little brothers in the house, it's not always easy to find peace and quiet. And since reading isn't the easiest thing for me, I really, really need peace and quiet when I'm trying to read my Bible and understand what God's Word is saying to me. And let's be honest: sitting still for anything—especially reading—isn't exactly what I'm known for.

So what's a can't-sit-still girl in a house with busy, noisy brothers supposed to do? Complain to Mom, of course! And do you know what she said? "Go outside!" And it worked! Maybe it was the warm sunshine or the breeze or the birds singing, but it was much more peaceful and way easier for me to sit still and concentrate. And I have to say there's something extra amazing about reading God's Word when I'm actually out in the world that He made.

Now on sunny days I love to head out and find a shady spot under the tree to read. When it's colder outside or a bit rainy, I'll climb up in the loft of the barn or hide away in a corner of the porch. It really doesn't matter where. I just know that for me, being outside helps me understand that God really is *God*. He's big and powerful and in control . . . and He's just waiting to talk to me through His Word.

Get outside with God's Word today, and see how He speaks to you.

## A BRAVE GIRL'S PRAYER

Lord, lead me to a special place where I can sit and read and listen and know that You are God. Amen.

Glory

# MORE THAN YOU CAN IMAGINE

With God's power working in us, God can do much, much more than anything we can ask or imagine.

—EPHESIANS 3:20 NCV

This past weekend the youth group went to serve a meal and hand out warm scarves at a homeless shelter. And I'll be honest: it was a little intimidating for me. I wasn't sure I would know what to say or do around people who were so different from me. I even thought about not going, but I decided to ask God for help instead. I prayed that He would help me do what He wanted me to do.

It didn't take long to realize those people weren't so different. Sure, they looked different and dressed different. And some of them struggled in ways I didn't understand. But really, they wanted the same basic things I wanted—to have food and warm clothes and a safe place to sleep and to live. God helped me see that He made and loves each of these people. And I found myself talking to them just like I would to the Brave Girls.

Whenever you need to do something—something you know is good but that's hard for you—remember this: God never asks us to do anything on our own. He goes before us, making sure we have whatever we need in order to do what He wants us to do. We're never alone. And He works through us to shine the light of His love into the world.

When we work together with God, we can do much more than we could ever do on our own—more than we could ever even imagine.

## A BRAVE GIRL'S PRAYER

Lord, work through me today to do things I never even imagined. Amen.

# COZY NO-SEW SCARF

These scarves are not only warm but so easy to make too.
Make a bunch to give as gifts or to give to a shelter.

**TIME: 1 HOUR TO MAKE ALL 3 SCARVES**

## MATERIALS

1 yard (1 m) of fleece fabric

## TOOLS

fabric scissors

long straight edge, such as a
   yardstick or meterstick

## STEPS

1. Make sure the edges of your fabric are straight. (Sometimes the edge cut at the store will be ragged.) If needed, use a straight edge to mark a straight line and trim. If there is white or curled fabric along one edge, cut that off in a straight line as well.

2. From the straight edge of the fabric, measure and mark 12 inches (30 cm). Moving down the fabric, mark 12 inches (30 cm) in at least three places to create a cutting line. Repeat twice more, measuring 12 inches (30 cm) from the previous line, to create two more lines.

3. Cut the fleece along your marks to make three strips.

4. Make cuts 4 inches (10 cm) deep and half an inch (1.5 cm) apart all across the two narrow ends of the scarf. This will make the fringe.

5. Tie each strip of the fringe in a knot.

Gracie

DAY 57

# A GOOD NIGHT FOR a GOOD MORNING

Do your planning and prepare.
—PROVERBS 24:27 NLT

Like I said before, getting up in the morning is *not* on my list of favorite things to do. So I've tried to come up with ways to make it better. And one of the best ways I've found to have a good morning is to start the night before. I know that if I leave myself too many things to do in the morning, I'm sure to forget something—or be so rushed and stressed that it gets my day off to a terrible start. A little bit of planning and preparation the night before makes the mornings *so* much better. Here's what I do:

- Lay out my clothes and shoes for the next day.

- Gather up homework, permission slips, and anything else I'll need and put them in my backpack.

- Gather up any special things for after-school activities or practices.

- Set my alarm for the next morning.

- Read my Bible to get my thoughts headed in the right direction.

- Talk to God about my day and ask Him to guide me through tomorrow.

Getting everything ready the night before helps me so much in the mornings. I don't have to worry if I've forgotten anything because I've planned ahead. I especially love talking to God right before I go to sleep. I put everything I'm worried about in His hands—and I trust Him to take care of me.

What could you do in the evenings to make your mornings better?

## A BRAVE GIRL'S PRAYER

Dear God, thank You for always being there to watch over me—even while I sleep. Amen.

Gracie

# GOOD MORNING

*Joy comes in the morning.*

—PSALM 30:5 NCV

Getting up in the morning is not my favorite thing to do. I'd much rather dive back under the covers and sleep a little more! But with school, that's not really an option.

I used to force myself to get up and get moving. I'd scramble for something to wear and try to find my homework. And I'd feel so stressed as I rushed out the door. Tired of my miserable mornings, I decided to figure out a way to actually *enjoy* my mornings. Crazy, right? But it actually works!

What's my secret? I created a routine to get me up and going with a smile. (It actually starts the night before because, let's face it, my brain is still a bit sleepy—even with the new routine! Check out the previous devotion for what to do at night.) Here's what works for me:

1. Before I even get out of bed—I smile and say, "Good morning, God!" After all, talking to God is always something to smile about.
2. I get washed up and dressed.
3. I choose a verse from my favorite verses collection to read and think about through the day. (I'll show you how to make your own collection a bit later.)
4. I eat breakfast.
5. I grab my backpack, and then I'm out the door—with a smile on my face!

My routine gives me a joy-filled start to a joyful day. Give it a try by creating your own morning routine—and set yourself up for joy in the mornings.

### A BRAVE GIRL'S PRAYER

Dear God, thank You for mornings—help me discover the joy in every morning!

# FAVORITE VERSES COLLECTION

Start a collection of your favorite verses to treasure
and inspire you your whole life through.

**TIME: 15 MINUTES**

## MATERIALS

box to hold the cards (a recipe box works wonderfully)

markers, colored pencils, paints, stickers, or jewels (optional)

favorite Bible verses

index cards

pencil or pen

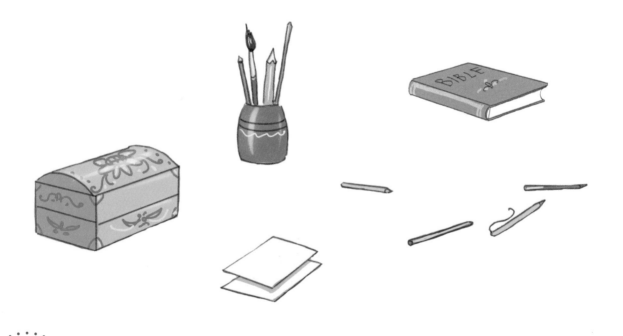

## STEPS

1. If you want to make the box fancier, decorate it with permanent marker drawings, paint, stickers, jewels, or anything you'd like.

2. Write your favorite verses on index cards. Decorate each card.

3. Tuck your cards into the box.

4. Whenever you come across another verse that touches your heart, add it to your collection.

5. Draw out one card each morning, and focus on that verse throughout the day.

DAY 59

# DO YOU

The Father has loved us so much that we are called children of God.
—1 JOHN 3:1 NCV

It wasn't that long ago that I skipped a grade in school. And while getting to learn new things was awesome, I quickly discovered that being one of the youngest kids in my grade wasn't going to be easy.

For a while I tried fitting in with the cool crowd. I tried wearing the "right" clothes—which turned out to be all wrong for me. (Glory's the one with the fashion sense. But me? Let's just say I'm better at color-coordinating my notes and pens than my clothes!) I also tried talking like some of the older kids too, even saying a few things I knew I shouldn't. Mostly, I guess I tried not being . . . me.

And that didn't work *at all*. I was miserable because I wasn't being faithful to who God said I was—His beloved child. Fortunately, the other Brave Girls helped me remember that I'm amazing because that's the way God made me. And once I stopped trying to be someone I wasn't, I actually had a lot of fun being *me*.

When you're thrown into a situation and you're tempted to try to be like someone else, remember who God says you are—His own amazing child. Try memorizing 1 John 3:1, and let it remind you to have fun just being the wonderful *you* God created.

## A BRAVE GIRL'S PRAYER

Dear God, give me the confidence to enjoy being who You made me to be. Amen.

Glory

# A DROP IN THE BUCKET

LORD our Lord, your name is the most wonderful name in all the earth!

—PSALM 8:9 NCV

There's something about the ocean that makes me feel close to God. Maybe because it's always there, day after day, and it reminds me that God is always there too. Or maybe it's because I know that since God is big enough and powerful enough to create all of that, then He is certainly big enough and powerful enough to take care of little me.

Some people look at things like the ocean, and they feel small and unimportant. They wonder, *What am I compared to something so huge?* Did you know that David asked the same question in Psalm 8? He looked at the wonders of creation all around him and asked God, "Why are people even important to you? Why do you take care of human beings?" (v. 4).

David didn't ask that question because he doubted that he was important to God though. David was amazed by just how important he was—how important we all are—to the One who created everything. David marveled at how God made us "a little lower than the angels and crowned [us] with glory and honor" (v. 5). And David remembered that God put us in charge of His creation, from "birds in the sky" to "fish in the sea" (v. 8).

So when I look out at that great big ocean and see it stretching farther than I can see, I think, *Wow! This is only a drop in the bucket compared to how much God loves me!*

Do you have a place where it's easy to feel close to God? Why does it make you feel that way?

## A BRAVE GIRL'S PRAYER

Lord, thank You for the wonders of Your creation—and especially for the wonder of how much You love me! Amen.

Gracie

# ASK

"Ask and you will receive, so that your joy
will be the fullest possible joy."

—JOHN 16:24 NCV

By now you might have heard that we can ask God for anything. Of course, that doesn't mean He'll give us *everything* we ask for. (Okay, so maybe I don't really need that new scooter in three different colors.) God *does* promise to give us exactly what we need though. Which is pretty wonderful, right?

Did you know that one of the things we can ask for is joy? I remember when my dad lost his job and our family was really struggling. It was hard not having enough money. Then I found this verse about "ask and you will receive," so I asked. I asked for my dad to get a job. I asked for my family not to have to move again. I also asked for joy . . . because I wasn't feeling much of it. And do you know what? God answered! It took a little while for my dad to get a new job, but he did. While we were waiting, God helped me see all the good that was coming out of this tough time—like how we worked together as a family and how we were extra careful to encourage my dad.

Have you ever asked God for joy? Why not give it a try? Write out your own prayer. Ask Him to help you see the happiness that He puts into every day. Because I promise you, when God is in your life, there's always something to smile about.

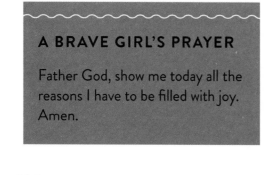

## A BRAVE GIRL'S PRAYER

Father God, show me today all the reasons I have to be filled with joy. Amen.

# LOOK AT THE FLOWERS

"Look at the wild flowers. See how they grow. They don't work or make clothes for themselves. But I tell you that even Solomon, the great and rich king, was not dressed as beautifully as one of these flowers."

—LUKE 12:27 ICB

Whenever I see a flower, I just have to stop and take a closer look. I guess that's because they help me remember God's promises. You see, God tells us that if we're ever worried about food or clothes or anything at all, we should look at the flowers. It's easy to see how much God loves them by how beautiful they all are. But just think about it: if God takes the time and the care to make flowers so amazing—flowers that can't ever love Him back—just imagine how much more He will do for us, His children!

God promises to give us everything we need (Philippians 4:19) and to bless us with His own love and care. But sometimes we have to wait on it—and that's never easy, is it? When I'm waiting on God, I like to look at flowers to help me remember that He really will answer. In fact, I kind of fill up my life with them. I sketch them and paint them. I pick them and tuck them into the pages of my books and my Bible. I even make a special kind of art from their petals—I'll teach you how. For me, filling up my art and my life with flowers is such a pretty way to remember that God keeps His promises. What reminds you of God's faithful promise-keeping?

## A BRAVE GIRL'S PRAYER

Lord, thank You for flowers. Help me always trust that You will keep Your promise to take care of me. Amen.

# NATURE'S ART

Capture the beauty of God's flower and plant creations with this unique art method.

TIME: 15–30 MINUTES, PLUS TIME TO GATHER FLOWERS AND LEAVES

## MATERIALS

fresh flowers and leaves

1 large paper bag or sheet of parchment paper

1 sheet white cardstock paper

paper towels

## TOOLS

plastic cutting board

scissors

safety goggles

hammer

tweezers

Experiment with different kinds of leaves and flowers, or try layering more flowers on top of your print (letting your paper dry between each layer).

## STEPS

1. Gather fresh flowers and leaves. Look for ones that are brightly colored.

2. Cover the cutting board with the paper bag or parchment paper.

3. Place a sheet of cardstock on the cutting board.

4. Arrange the leaves and flowers on the cardstock. Use the scissors to cut off any extra thick parts that might be too "juicy," such as stems. (For thicker flowers, you may want to pull off the petals and arrange them on the paper.)

5. Cover with three layers of paper towels.

6. Put on the goggles, and then use the hammer to firmly tap across your paper. Work your way back and forth across the paper until you've hammered every bit of the flowers and leaves.

7. Gently lift up the paper towel. If the colors have transferred to the paper towel, remove the towel. If they haven't, replace the paper towel and hammer some more.

8. Use the tweezers to remove the flowers and leaves. (If the flowers stick, let them dry and then brush them off.)

Voilà! Nature's art!

Honor

DAY 63

# GOD IN, GOD OUT

Think about the things that are good and worthy of praise. Think about the things that are true and honorable and right and pure and beautiful and respected.

—PHILIPPIANS 4:8 NCV

I've been taking this computer class at school, and I learned a new term: GIGO. It stands for *garbage in, garbage out.* It basically means that whatever you put into your computer program is what you'll get out. If you put in bad coding and commands, you'll get a bad program that doesn't work. Of course, the opposite is also true: if you put in good coding, you'll get a good program that does just what you told it to.

That started me thinking . . . maybe GIGO doesn't apply only to computers; maybe it applies to us too. The Bible talks a lot about being careful of the things we look at, listen to, read, and think about. What if that's because what we put into ourselves is what we'll get out? For me, I know that when I'm focusing on the good things in my life and on the goodness of God, I'm a lot happier than when I'm focusing on all the bad and wrong stuff in the world.

We need to fill our thoughts with those things that are good—and what could be better than God? Maybe we should create our own definition of GIGO: God in, God out! Because when we pour God into our thoughts, He spills out into our lives.

How can you pour God into your life today? Maybe memorize a favorite verse, learn a new praise song, or write out a prayer to Him.

## A BRAVE GIRL'S PRAYER

Lord, fill my thoughts with all the things that make You smile. Amen.

Hope

# A LITTLE DIRT NEVER HURT

*"I have given you an example to follow. Do as I have done to you."*

—JOHN 13:15 NLT

When you live on a farm, there's dirt everywhere—in the fields, in the barn, in the woods, around the animals. And sooner or later, some of that dirt is bound to get on you. Especially when you're out riding bikes on dusty roads or diving into hay bales or helping out in the garden. But as my mom and dad say, a little dirt never hurt anyone.

When you think about it, Jesus wasn't afraid of a little dirt either. He walked dusty roads, had picnics on the beach, and hung out on fishing boats. He drew in the dirt with His finger when some Pharisees tried to trap Him with their words (John 8:1–11). He even washed His own disciples' dirty feet! And then He said, "I have given you an example to follow. Do as I have done to you."

Serving God isn't always neat and clean and tidy. It isn't always dressed up and shiny for church either. Sometimes it's scrubbing pots after serving dinner at a shelter or changing diapers in the nursery or helping plant a tree at a children's home. Serving God can get a little messy! And if Jesus wasn't afraid to get a little dirty, why should we be? How can you get a little messy serving Jesus today?

## A BRAVE GIRL'S PRAYER

Lord, show me how I can serve You today—and help me remember that a little dirt never hurt. Amen.

# PLANT A TREE

You might get a little messy with this activity, but you'll enjoy the results of your work for years to come!

TIME: 1 HOUR (PLUS SHOPPING TIME)

## MATERIALS

1-gallon (4-L) pot holding a small tree native to your area

## TOOLS

gardening gloves

shovel

watering can or hose

Take pictures to track how fast your tree grows and how it changes through the seasons.

## STEPS

1. Take a family field trip to a local nursery to pick out a tree. Ask a worker which kind of tree is best to plant where you live and how much water and sunlight it needs.

2. Pick a spot for your tree that gets the right amount of sunlight and has room for your tree to grow.

3. Dig a hole as deep as the pot and two to three times wider than the pot.

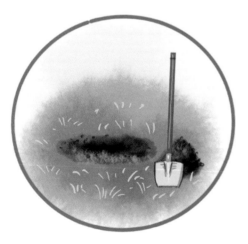

4. Put on the gardening gloves, and remove the tree from the pot. Loosen the roots and spread them out a bit.

5. Place the tree in the hole.

6. Fill in the hole with dirt, breaking up any big clods.

7. Thoroughly water the tree.

For the next year, be careful to keep your tree watered (but not soaked), especially if the weather is dry.

DAY 65

# FUN FOR ALL AGES

GRAY HAIR is a CROWN of glory; it is gained by living a godly life.
—PROVERBS 16:31 NLT

How many of the older people at your church do you really know? I have to admit that it's all too easy for me to look at them and see only the gray hair, the wrinkles, the canes. And I think, *I don't have anything in common with them.* Or at least that's what I used to think. Now I know better!

You see, our youth group started hosting a board game night for senior citizens one night a month. First, we teach them one of our favorite games, and then they teach us one of theirs. They've shown me games I'd never even heard of—the games they played when they were my age. And they creamed me at some of the games I *thought* I was really good at playing. It seems that every month I laugh so hard that my sides hurt!

It didn't take long for me and the other Brave Girls to realize that there's more to people than how old they are. These grandmas and grandpas turned out to be some of the craziest, funniest, best people I've ever hung out with. I stopped seeing gray hair and wrinkles and canes, and I started seeing friends. Now I find myself looking forward to visiting with them each week at church.

Ask your parents or youth group leader if you can host a game night for the senior citizens at your church. You might be surprised by how many new friends you'll meet!

## A BRAVE GIRL'S PRAYER

Holy Father, help me see that friends come in all ages and stages of life. Amen.

# Rainy Days

This is the day the LORD has made. We will rejoice and be glad in it.

—PSALM 118:24 NLT

Plip, plip, plop. Drip, drip, drop. That's the rain falling outside my window right now. I know a lot of people dread rainy days, but me? I love them. Seriously! That's because rainy days remind me of how amazing God is.

Sure, it would be easy to focus on the mud and the puddles, but just think how much fun they are to splash in! And when a storm roars through, I think about Jesus standing up in that boat and telling that storm to hush and be quiet. I love snuggling down into my blanket and knowing I'm safe inside my house—kind of like I'm safe inside Jesus' love, no matter how big or loud the storms in this world get.

And after the rain passes, there are so many wonders to enjoy—like the way the sunlight sparkles on the grass and the leaves. It seems the whole world is covered with glitzy diamonds. Sometimes there's even a rainbow, and I'm reminded of all God's promises.

The next time you find yourself dreading a rainy day, don't focus on the mud and the puddles. Instead, count all the beautiful and amazing things God has hidden inside even the rainiest of days. Oh . . . and don't forget to go splash through a puddle or two!

### A BRAVE GIRL'S PRAYER

Lord, teach me to see the beauty You have put in each day, especially rainy days. Amen.

DAY 67

# START SMALL

Good people take care of their animals.

—PROVERBS 12:10 NCV

For me, there's not much that's better than playing with puppies and kittens. I guess that's why I love the days when my family goes to help out at the animal shelter. Sometimes I help give the animals food and water. Other times I take them for a walk or play with them. And yeah, sometimes I clean up after them, and that's okay too.

What I *really* want to do is gather up all the animals at the shelter and take them home with me. But I can't do that. Sadly, there are just too many of them. What I can do is make sure they have a fun day when I come to help out.

There are times when we see big problems in the world—like all the homeless pets—and we feel like we can't really do anything about them. What I'm learning, though, is that I can start small, and I can make a difference right where I am. And you can too!

Check with your local animal shelter to see how you and your family can help out. Or if animals aren't your thing, check with a nearby retirement home, talk to a single parent at church who could use a babysitter, or check for litter cleanup days in your neighborhood. No matter what you like, there's a way to help out and have fun doing it!

## A BRAVE GIRL'S PRAYER

Lord, show me how I can make a difference right where I am. Amen.

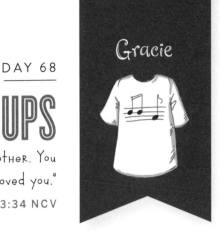

Gracie

# PICK-ME-UPS

"I give you a new command: Love each other. You must love each other as I have loved you."

—JOHN 13:34 NCV

We all need a pick-me-up once in a while. Everyone has rough days, sick days, and just long days. That's one thing I love about the Brave Girls—we pick each other up on all the kinds of days.

Of course, I had friends at my old school back in Pennsylvania, but we never really did that for each other. I think following God is what makes the difference. When we realize how much He loves us and how much He wants us to love each other, we just have to do something about it. Like when I first moved here, Glory gave me the prettiest little notepad with her phone number written at the top. Not only was it a thoughtful gift, but it let me know I really wasn't all alone in this new town—I had a friend in the making.

Now, whenever one of us is in need of a pick-me-up, we'll offer a hug, send a text, or give her a little gift. Nothing huge—just something to let her know we're thinking of her. And we don't just do it for our own little group either. We give pick-me-ups to other friends, neighbors, our families, a teacher, our pastor, and our youth group leader. And it doesn't have to be when they're having a bad day. After all, every day is a good day for a little pick-me-up from a friend.

One of my favorite pick-me-ups to give (and to get!) is a cookie my mom taught me to make. Give it a try—and be sure to share with a friend.

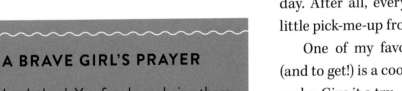

### A BRAVE GIRL'S PRAYER

Lord, thank You for always being there when I need a pick-me-up! Amen.

121

# PICK-ME-UP COOKIES

These yummy, no-bake peanut butter and chocolate cookies are easy to make and perfect for sharing! Tuck in a note that says, "God's got you—and you've got this!"

Be sure to ask a grown-up to help you with the stove.

**TOTAL TIME: 50 MINUTES**

**COOK TIME: 20 MINUTES**

**COOL TIME: 30 MINUTES**

**MAKES: 2 DOZEN**

## INGREDIENTS

2 cups (400 g) sugar

4 tablespoons (60 g) cocoa

½ cup (120 ml) milk

½ cup butter (113 g) or margarine, cut into chunks

½ cup (125 g) peanut butter

1 teaspoon (5 ml) vanilla extract

3 cups (270 g) quick-cooking oats

## TOOLS

medium-size, nonstick saucepan

silicone spatula

measuring cups and spoons

wax paper

Place these cookies in a homemade basket to make a special gift. See the basket directions after Day 86.

## STEPS

1. In the saucepan, stir together the sugar, cocoa, milk, and butter.

2. Heat over medium-high heat until the mixture boils. Boil for 3 minutes, stirring often.

3. Remove from heat. Stir in peanut butter until melted.

4. Mix in vanilla.

5. Stir in oats, 1 cup at a time.

6. Drop by large spoonfuls onto wax paper. Work quickly before the mixture cools.

7. Let cookies cool for 30 minutes or until set.

DAY 69

# LAUGH A LITTLE . . . OR A LOT!

*We were filled with laughter, and we sang happy songs.*
—PSALM 126:2 NCV

Did you hear the one about the barber who won the race? Yeah, he knew a short cut. Do you know why the golfer wore two pairs of pants? In case he got a hole in one! Oh, and one more . . . do you know why corn is such a good listener? Because it's all ears!

Okay, so maybe those jokes were a little corny. (Ha ha! I couldn't resist!) But I'll bet they made you giggle, or at least smile a little bit. And for just a second, everything seemed right with the world. That's the power of laughter. Whether it's a teeny, tiny little giggle or a great big, gigantic belly laugh, laughter has the power to make a good day even better and a tough day not quite so tough.

My dad has at least a million of these cheesy jokes stored up inside his brain. Whenever one of us is sad or mad or we've just had a bad day, he starts pulling them out. And the next thing we know, we're laughing. There still might be things to be mad or sad about, but a little laughter seems to make them easier to handle. The next time you see a friend having a mad, sad, or bad day, ask her this question: What do you call a pile of cats? A *meow*ntain.

And here's one last one . . . why can't your nose be twelve inches long? Because then it would be a foot! Tell a friend a joke today.

### A BRAVE GIRL'S PRAYER

Lord, thank You for the gift of laughter and the power it has to make life a little less tough. Amen.

Glory

# ON WITH THE SHOW!

I will speak using stories. . . . We will tell about
His power and the miracles He has done.
—PSALM 78:2, 4 ICB

A little while ago, our pastor asked the Brave Girls to watch a group of younger kids while the adults had a meeting at church. The kids were all different ages, so we needed something everyone would enjoy. We put our heads together and came up with the idea of doing a skit. Everyone would enjoy that, including us!

We chose to do the story of Esther because we love stories about ladies saving the day. The first thing we did was write a script. We used the Bible to get the facts right, and then we added some dialogue—and a few funnies to make the kids laugh.

I gathered up odds and ends for costumes and props, and we even made a few things ourselves, like Esther's and King Xerxes' crowns. We spent a couple of afternoons rehearsing, and then it was showtime. We were a hit! The kids giggled and laughed—and learned a lot about how Esther saved the Jews' lives by speaking up.

When the show was over, the kids took turns borrowing our costumes and acting out the skit for themselves. We also brainstormed how we can speak up and stand up for others in our everyday lives. Afterward the children's minister asked us to do an encore performance in Bible class the next week. So I guess you could say we're taking this show on the road!

Skits are a fun way to learn what the Bible says and share it with others. What message has God put in His Word that you can act out in a skit—or in real life?

## A BRAVE GIRL'S PRAYER

Lord, help me tell the world how wonderful You are! Amen.

# SKIT TIPS & TRICKS

Skits are great ways to teach about the Bible and about living a brave life. And bonus—they're fun for everyone!

## MATERIALS

a story to act out

a place to hold the performance

actors

costumes and props

an audience

> If you mess up or forget a line, just make something up and keep going— that's what the pros do. The audience will never know!

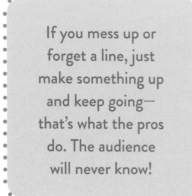

## STEPS

1. Write out a Bible story or create your own story that teaches a lesson like giving, helping others, or forgiving.

2. Decide how many actors you'll need and divide out the parts.

3. Decide what costumes and props you will need. Then gather, collect, and create! Make your supplies as simple or as fancy as you like.

4. Think about who you want to perform your skit for and where you'll perform it. Your skit might be for a Sunday school class or Vacation Bible School. It could be for family and friends or the whole neighborhood.

5. Create a playbill—a piece of paper to hand out to everyone that tells the name of the play and who will be playing each part.

6. Rehearse! Rehearse! Rehearse!

7. On the day of the performance, step out to tell your audience the name of the skit— and then it's on with the show!

8. After the performance, gather all the actors together to take a great big bow!

### No-Sew Bible Times Robe

Take a large piece of fabric and fold it in half. When it's folded in half longways, it should be long enough to reach from your shoulders to your ankles. (Knit fabric is best because it won't unravel.) Cut a half circle in the folded edge to make a hole for your head. Then simply slip it over your head, add a belt—and ta-da!

A scarf makes a great belt for your robe. Or wrap a scarf around your head for a head covering.

DAY 71

# IT'S FOR ME

Your word is a lamp to guide my feet and a light for my path.
—PSALM 119:105 NLT

You may have heard before that the Bible is actually a love letter from God to all people, everywhere, and in all times. But the Bible isn't *just* a love letter to everyone; it's a love letter to me and to you *personally*.

There's a verse in 2 Timothy that says that all Scripture is "God-breathed" (3:16 NIV). And sometimes, when I sit down with my Bible in my special quiet place, it *is* as if He is whispering the words straight to me. But sometimes the words don't click as well. When that happens, I have a simple trick to help me remember that God's words really are for me: I make them my own by actually putting *my* name in the verse, like this:

"For God so loved *Faith* that he gave his one and only Son" (from John 3:16).

Try it with your name. Do you feel the difference? Sometimes I even write it that way in my Bible so that I'll see my name whenever I read that verse and remember that God's promises are for *me*. Here are some of my other favorite verses to personalize:

- Isaiah 41:13

- Jeremiah 29:11

- Philippians 4:19

What are your favorite verses? Write them out and add in your name to help you remember God's Word is His letter of love to *you*.

## A BRAVE GIRL'S PRAYER

Lord, You are so big and powerful and amazing, and yet You know and love me personally. Thank You! Amen.

# MAKE TIME FOR GOD

*Use every chance you have for doing good.*

—EPHESIANS 5:16 NCV

I wanted to share with you a struggle I've been having—and a way I've figured out to fix it. I've had so much going on with church, school, homework, youth group, science club, debate team, *and* my work at the animal shelter. Not to mention hanging out with my friends and family. One day I realized I had been so busy that I hadn't talked to God *in days*!

Something had to change. So I did what I always do when I have a problem to solve: I headed for the library. I checked out all these books on time management, and the biggest thing I learned was how to use a calendar to keep track of everything. And since time with God is something I *definitely* need, I made sure to include time for Him every day.

First, I made a checklist of the things I want to do every day: pray, list three things I'm thankful for, and read at least one Bible chapter. Then I made a list of other things I can do for God—one for each day of the week. After that, I added in all my activities and responsibilities. It took a little getting used to, but now it's such a huge help! Now, because I put God on my calendar first, I always have time for Him.

Do you ever struggle to make time for God? Give the calendar a try—it's really helped me!

## A BRAVE GIRL'S PRAYER

Lord, help me remember that making time for You is the most important thing I can do. Amen.

# BRAVE LIFE PLANNER

Writing things down on a calendar helps us remember the things we need to do—and nothing is more important than remembering to be faithful to God! Make a Brave Life Planner to help you remember to live brave every day.

Make a daily checklist to help you remember to do the most important things each week. Each Sunday fill in your planner for the next week by starting with your weekly checklist. Then add the rest of the week's items, such as tests, sports practice, and family events. Whenever you learn of a new event or task, add it to your planner right away.

## this week . . . . .

**Monday:** memorize a Bible verse
**Tuesday:** text or write an encouraging note
**Wednesday:** worship
**Thursday:** talk to someone about Jesus
**Friday:** pray for someone who is going through a rough time
**Saturday:** serve someone
**Sunday:** share a Bible verse with someone

tuesday

Science test
tomorrow!

text an
encouraging
note to Glory

clean out
rabbit cage

Daily Checklist        Thankful for...
                       1.
☐ pray                 2.
☐ Read daily devotional 3.
☐

VOLUNTEER

BIBLE

Gracie

# MAKE GOD SING

"The Lord will be happy with you. You will rest in His love. He will sing and be joyful about you."

—ZEPHANIAH 3:17 ICB

It's no secret that I love to sing. I sing when I'm happy, when I'm sad, and even when I'm angry. I sing about God and friendship, sunny days and storms—all kinds of things. It doesn't take much to make me think of a song and start to sing. But I've noticed that it's the things that make me happy that most inspire me to let a song loose.

Maybe that's why I love this verse from Zephaniah—that book almost at the very end of the Old Testament that we forget about sometimes! It says, "The Lord will be happy with you. You will rest in his love. He will sing and be joyful about you."

Did you catch that? God sings about us! When God sees us living the way He wants us to live, it makes Him so happy and joyful that He just has to sing! Wouldn't you love to hear that? I guess we will in heaven someday. But for today, I want to do all I can to keep God singing. Don't get me wrong though. I've learned that God always loves us, no matter what. There's nothing we can do—good or bad—to change how much He loves us. But our actions *can* make Him happy or sad. So what can you do today to make God happy? What can you do to make Him sing?

## A BRAVE GIRL'S PRAYER

Lord, teach me to live a life that makes You sing! Amen.

Hope

# REAPING AND SOWING

*A man reaps what he sows. . . . Let us not become weary in doing good, for at the proper time we will reap a harvest if we do not give up.*
—GALATIANS 6:7, 9 NIV

When you live on a farm, there's usually either reaping or sowing going on. And if you don't live on a farm, you might be thinking, *Hope, what are you talking about?* Well, let's start with sowing. *Sowing* means planting seeds. *Reaping* is harvesting what grows from the seeds. So if you sow corn seeds, you will reap corn. If you sow watermelon seeds, you will reap watermelons. And if you want strawberries, you should definitely *not* plant apple seeds. You get the idea.

Farms aren't the only places where you reap what you sow. It happens in life too. We usually think of this in bad ways—like if we sow anger, we'll reap anger. But I've found that it also works in good ways. If we sow seeds of kindness, we'll reap lots of kindness in our day. If we sow love, we'll get love in return. And sowing smiles will give you a harvest of smiles.

Some people expect to reap good friendships even while they're sowing things like jealousy, gossip, or even meanness. That just will *not* work. If you're looking for a harvest of good friends, make sure you're sowing good seeds of kindness, love, and smiles. Besides, sowing those kinds of seeds is much more fun!

## A BRAVE GIRL'S PRAYER

Lord, help me make sure I'm planting seeds of goodness, kindness, and love. Amen.

Glory

DAY 75

# Get up and Move!

You should know that your body is a temple for the Holy Spirit who is in you.

—1 CORINTHIANS 6:19 NCV

Do you ever feel like you're walking through mud? Like just putting one foot in front of the other takes everything you've got? Or maybe all you can think about is curling up and taking a nap, even though it's only nine thirty in the morning. I call that feeling "draggy." My mom calls it "sluggish." But my dad calls it "time to get up and move." He says God gave arms and legs and feet for a reason: He *made* us to move.

So whenever I complain about feeling draggy, my dad will make this goofy trumpeting sound and announce, "Time to get up and move!" Then he'll crank up one of his favorite old songs (which aren't *too* terrible), grab my hand, and start dancing around the room. And even though *moving* is usually the absolute last thing I want to do, it actually . . . works. Before I even realize it, that draggy feeling is gone.

The thing is that our bodies weren't just made to move; they *need* to move in order to stay healthy. And remember, as a follower of Jesus, God's Spirit lives inside you—so it's His house too. Be sure to keep it in shape.

The next time you're feeling sluggish or draggy, get up off the couch. Go for a ride on your scooter or bike, take a walk or swim, or get up and dance. But turning on one of your parents' old tunes is completely up to you!

## A BRAVE GIRL'S PRAYER

Thank You, Lord, for a body that can do so many things. I want to take care of it. Amen.

Faith

# MY PRAYING PLACE

Jesus often slipped away to be alone so He could pray.

—LUKE 5:16 NCV

I want to let you in on a little secret: I absolutely *love* my family and friends, but sometimes I need to get away and be alone with God. And actually that's a good thing. The Bible tells us that even Jesus would slip away sometimes to be alone with His Father. And if Jesus needed to do that, then I know I do!

My mom helped me set up a special place in the corner of my room. First we dragged in an old chair. It wasn't very pretty, but it was super comfortable. And when we covered it with a big, cozy quilt we already had, it looked just fine. We found a little table at a yard sale for only $3 and put that next to the chair. I added a lamp, a jar filled with pens and pencils, my journal, and of course, my Bible.

I try to spend a little time there each day, reading my Bible and talking to God. I also like to journal—I get writing ideas from my journal jar. (I'll tell you how to make one for yourself on the next page.)

You should try setting up your own special place to be alone with God. It could be a chair or a big stack of pillows in the corner of your room. Or it could be outside on a porch swing or even up in a tree. Anywhere you can be alone with God is the perfect spot to be.

## A BRAVE GIRL'S PRAYER

Lord, I thank You for being a God who wants to be with me. Amen.

# JOURNAL JAR

This idea-filled jar is a pretty and practical way to help with journal writing. Make one for yourself and for a friend.

TIME: 30 MINUTES

## MATERIALS

pretty paper

pencil or pen

clear, clean jar with a lid

18-inch (46-cm) ribbon

## TOOLS

scissors

## STEPS

1. Cut the paper into strips large enough to write your ideas on.

2. Write one journal prompt on each strip. Create your own, use the ones suggested here, or both!

3. Fold and place the paper inside the jar.

4. Add the lid and tie on a pretty ribbon.

5. Whenever you need an idea for journaling, pull out a piece of paper and start writing!

# JOURNALING IDEAS

I saw God's love . . .

Something I wish I had done . . .

Friendship is . . .

Being brave means . . .

I want to be better at . . .

It was amazing when . . .

My favorite verse is ____ because . . .

The song I love . . .

I want to praise God for . . .

My faith means . . .

I want to share God's love . . .

In the future, I want to be more . . .

One thing I want to tell my mom . . .

One thing I want to tell my dad . . .

I want to be ____ for my friends so that . . .

A friend I want to pray for . . .

If I could ask God anything . . .

Three things I want to do this year are . . .

I am so thankful for . . .

I want to be ____ for God so that . . .

Gracie

# SING GOD'S WORD INTO YOUR HEART

I have hidden your word in my heart that I might not sin against you.

—PSALM 119:11 NIV

When I first started learning about being God's girl, I read this verse about hiding God's Word in my heart. I asked our Sunday school teacher what that meant, and she said that to hide God's Word in my heart was to memorize it. That way I would always have it with me. Even when I didn't have my Bible, His Word would help me do what was right and stay away from what was wrong. It would also give me joy and peace, she said. Well, that sounded great, but memorizing is not always easy—or fun—to do.

I was trying to figure out ways to make myself *want* to memorize God's Word when I noticed something. A lot of the praise songs we were singing in youth group and in church were actually Bible verses set to music. Memorizing might not be my favorite thing, but music is! So I started memorizing those songs. Then I had an idea: I could take the verses I wanted to memorize and turn them into songs. At first, I sang the words to tunes I already knew. Then I started making up my own tunes.

I've been able to memorize tons of verses—and I've had fun doing it. Give it a try. Pick out a verse you want to remember—one that's special to you. Set it to music and sing God's Word into your heart!

## A BRAVE GIRL'S PRAYER

God, Your Word is so rich and full of joy. Help me hide Your words in my heart. Amen.

Glory

DAY 78

# SWEET KINDNESS

*He comforts us every time we have trouble, so when others have trouble, we can comfort them with the same comfort God gives us.*

—2 CORINTHIANS 1:4 NCV

Every winter my mom and I make up a whole bunch of jars of hot chocolate mix. That way they're ready to give away to friends (and people we hope will become friends) who could use a little extra touch of kindness. The mix is super easy to make, so we try to always have a few jars in our pantry. My mom calls them hugs in a jar. Because when you're having a tough time, isn't it so comforting to get a simple gift that says someone is thinking of you? It's kind of like a warm hug from someone who loves you. (And the chocolate part never hurts!)

I don't know about you, but I used to get stressed out over what to say when a friend was hurting. Whether it was because someone was sick or had passed away, or because they were just having a terrible day, I was always afraid I would say the wrong thing. I've learned that sometimes it's better to just let our hugs do the talking. Because when you're there for someone—to hug, to listen, or to hand them a cup of hot chocolate—your presence is a sweet kindness they won't forget.

Who do you know who could use some sweet kindness today?

## A BRAVE GIRL'S PRAYER

Lord, thank You for all the times You comfort me. Help me see when someone else needs a bit of Your love and kindness. Amen.

# HUG IN A JAR

TIME: 20 MINUTES

MAKES: 1 PINT JAR (4 DRINKS)

## INGREDIENTS

1½ cups (125 g) instant nonfat dry milk

⅓ cup (65 g) sugar

6 tablespoons (90 g) baking cocoa

½ cup (27 g) miniature marshmallows

## TOOLS

large bowl

measuring cups

whisk

funnel

pint-size (16-ounce; 473-ml) Mason jar (use a larger jar if you're adding
    marshmallows and chocolate chips)

festive muffin liner

pen

cardstock

ribbon

## STEPS

1. Add dry milk, sugar, and cocoa to a large bowl. Stir with a whisk until well combined.

2. Stir in marshmallows.

3. Use a funnel to pour the mixture into the jar. Place the muffin liner on top of the jar and put the lid on top, sealing tightly.

4. Write the following instructions on a piece of cardstock, and sign your name.

5. Tie the paper to the jar with the ribbon.

*hug in a cup*

Spoon ½ cup cocoa mix into a mug.
Stir in 1 cup hot water or milk.

♡ GLORY

DAY 79

# A GReaT IDea

Do not let anyone treat you as if you are unimportant because you are young. Instead, be an example to the believers with your words, your actions, your love, your faith, and your pure life.

—1 TIMOTHY 4:12 NCV

The animal shelter had a big problem. They had rescued a bunch of new animals, so they needed more food, more medicine, more everything. But they didn't have enough money for all those things. My family and I gathered with all the other volunteers to figure out a way to raise the money. I had an idea, but I wasn't sure all those grown-ups would listen to me. I whispered my idea to my dad, and he said I should tell the whole group.

Honestly, I wasn't sure if I could do that. What if they thought it was silly? But then I remembered all those animals that needed help. So I said a quick prayer asking God to help me be brave, and then I raised my hand. The director asked me to stand and speak. I was so nervous that my knees were shaking! But I stood up anyway and said, "We could have a community dog wash right here. We already have the special tubs and shampoo. We could charge for each dog we wash and take donations too." Well, everyone loved my idea! We held the dog wash the very next weekend. The shelter raised so much money that the director said they might even make it a regular thing.

That day I learned that I may be young, but I still have great ideas worth sharing. And so do you! Don't let your age stop you from speaking up. Ask God to help you be brave—and He will.

## A BRAVE GIRL'S PRAYER

Lord, thank You for always being with me and helping me be brave. Amen.

# AN INVITATION

*"Here I am! I stand at the door and knock. If anyone hears my voice and opens the door, I will come in and eat with him. And he will eat with me."*

—REVELATION 3:20 ICB

The other day at church, I noticed an older lady sitting all by herself. I realized that I had seen her before and that she was always alone. After church in the parking lot, I saw her again. She was getting in her car, and she was still alone. It bothered me all the way home. And as I sat with my family around our big table, with everyone laughing and talking, I couldn't help but think about that lady. While we were washing dishes, I talked to my mom about it. I asked if we could invite the lady to lunch the next Sunday. So that's exactly what we did.

I wish you could have seen her face. She was *so* happy to be invited to lunch. It was just a simple lunch, nothing fancy. The house was even a little bit messy because it had been such a busy week. But she didn't mind a bit. And we had a wonderful time getting to know her. Since that day we have invited lots of people to join us for lunch—college students, widows, widowers, or just anyone who looks like they could use a friend.

There's something about sharing a meal and eating together that makes people instantly feel welcome. Maybe that's why Jesus so often shared a meal with others. Who can you invite to eat with you?

## A BRAVE GIRL'S PRAYER

Lord, show me someone I can make feel welcome today. Amen.

DAY 81

# WHAT DO YOU SEE?

[God] displays His power in the whirlwind and the storm.
The billowing clouds are the dust beneath His feet.

—NAHUM 1:3 NLT

One of my favorite things to do is stare up at the clouds. My mom calls it *cloud-gazing*. It's really easy. All you need to do is drag an old quilt or blanket out into the yard on a day when there are some clouds in the sky. Lie back on the blanket, and gaze up into the sky. How fast are the clouds moving? What direction are they going? What shapes do you see?

With a little imagination, you can see all sorts of things in the clouds—like a boat, a puppy, or a cow jumping over the moon. One of the craziest things I ever saw was a cloud shaped just like an elephant playing ball with a duck. (I told you it was crazy!)

What about God—do you see Him? Oh, I don't mean His face or anything like that! I mean, do you see how powerful He is? Remember, He is the One who created all the heavens, the skies, and the clouds. In fact, the Bible says that God is so big, the clouds are like "the dust beneath his feet."

The next time you see clouds in the sky, try a little cloud-gazing for yourself. And remember just how amazing God really is!

## A BRAVE GIRL'S PRAYER

Lord, I praise You for the clouds and the way they remind me of just how powerful and wonderful You are. Amen.

*Gracie*

# WHAT DOES GOD LOOK LIKE?

God is love.

—1 JOHN 4:8 NCV

I've learned a lot about Jesus since I became a part of the Brave Girls—like how Jesus came to earth to show us what God looks like. (That's in Colossians 1:15, by the way!) Okay, not what color hair He has or how tall or short He is. Jesus came to show us what God's *heart* looks like—and it looks like love.

You see, Jesus loved all people. He loved Mary and Joseph and His brothers and sisters. He loved the people who loved Him back, and the people who didn't even know Him. He loved the ones who followed Him and the ones who turned away from Him, like that rich, young ruler. He loved the people who did what they should and the people who did wrong. He even loved the Pharisees, who wanted to kill Him, and Judas, the one who betrayed Him.

Now that Jesus has gone up to heaven, He wants us to do what He did: show the world what God looks like. How? It's our job as Christians to show the world God's love. And not just to the people who look or think or act like us, but to *all* people. That means being kind to everyone, trying to always do what's right, helping when we can, and not thinking that we're better than anyone else. Jesus wants *you* to be the reason someone believes that He is good and loving. What can you do to show the world—or one person in it—that God is love today?

## A BRAVE GIRL'S PRAYER

God, thank You for loving me so very much. Help me love others the way You love me. Amen.

# DIY Decorated Mug

Add your own artistic touches to turn a plain mug into a thoughtful gift. Tuck in a note, a packet of tea or hot chocolate, and a little candy to create a gift that's sure to warm up anyone's day!

TIME: 1 HOUR

## MATERIALS

1 plain, light-colored ceramic mug

cotton balls and cotton swabs

rubbing alcohol

pencil

oil-based paint pens

## TOOLS

oven

## STEPS

1. Wash and dry your mug.

2. Dip a cotton ball in rubbing alcohol, and rub it over the mug. (This gets rid of any oils or residue.) Let it dry.

3. Sketch your design in pencil. You can write a name, a word, or a short Scripture. Or draw a picture or pattern.

4. On the bottom of the mug, write "Hand wash only" with a paint pen. (The dishwasher will chip off the paint.)

5. Paint over your design using the pens. If you make a mistake, simply rub it off with a cotton swab dipped in rubbing alcohol.

6. Place your painted mug in a cold oven, and set the temperature to 350 degrees Fahrenheit (177 degrees C). (Check with an adult about how to use the oven.)

7. When the oven has reached full temperature, bake for 30 minutes to set the paint. Turn off the oven, and leave your mug inside until it is cooled.

8. Fill your beautiful mug and give it away!

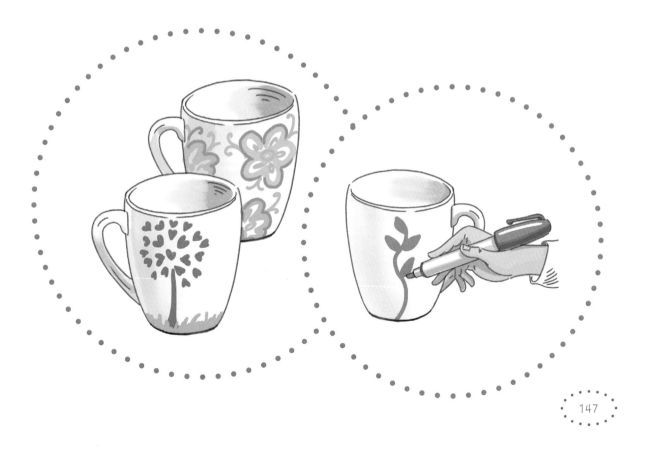

Honor

# THANKS FOR THE FROGS

God looked at everything He had made, and it was very good.
—GENESIS 1:31 NCV

Everybody knows I love animals. But what everybody doesn't realize is that I love *all* kinds of animals—not just cats and dogs and hamsters. I love the horses, cows, and chickens on Hope's farm. I love the crabs, fish, and seagulls we see when we go with Glory to the beach. I even love the spiders, snakes, and frogs I sometimes find right in my own backyard.

Some people think I'm a bit nutty for loving creatures like spiders and frogs. But the way I see it, God made those animals too. And they really are pretty amazing. I mean, a spider can spin its own sticky web to trap its dinner, but it doesn't get stuck in the web itself! And a frog can just shoot out its tongue to catch a snack. God made all these different kinds of creatures, and then He said they were all "good."

At first, you might wonder what "good" a spider could be. But just think of how many more bugs there would be if there weren't any spiders to eat them. (Even I have trouble admiring flies and mosquitoes—though I know God must have made them for a reason too.)

The next time you see a creature—one that isn't quite so cuddly as a puppy—take a minute and think about how amazing that creature really is. And then say "thank You" to God, who makes all creatures—including you and me!—"very good."

## A BRAVE GIRL'S PRAYER

Lord, thank You for the way You made this world and every creature in it so very good. Amen.

Glory

# Happy Terrific Tuesday Day!

THis is the day that the LoRD Has made. Let us Rejoice and be glad today!

—PSALM 118:24 NCV

I love special days! Birthdays, Christmas, Valentine's Day, Groundhog Day—it doesn't really matter what the special day is; it's just so wonderful to take a break from ordinary days. There's something about special days that helps me remember how blessed I am.

So when I woke up the other morning and I wasn't feeling particularly blessed, I decided I needed a special day to cheer me up. But it was a Tuesday. In September. Not a special day to celebrate in sight. Then I thought, *Wait a minute! Shouldn't every day with God be a special day?* So I declared that day to be "Happy Terrific Tuesday Day!" I skipped downstairs and announced the holiday to my mom—who promptly added sprinkles to my waffles. We listened to happy songs all the way to school, and I texted all my friends to wish them a Happy Terrific Tuesday! I even made a Happy Terrific Tuesday card in art class to hang on my mirror. It reminds me that every day is a day worth celebrating.

When we are followers of God, we have so many reasons to celebrate. Things like being loved and forgiven. Things like being able to talk to God anytime we want and knowing He will always hear us. So today, decide to celebrate your blessings. What will you call your special day?

## A BRAVE GIRL'S PRAYER

Lord, thank You for this day that You have made. Help me see all the joy You have put into it. Amen.

Hope

1

DAY 85

# IT'S GOING TO BE GREAT

*Always be joyful. Pray continually, and give thanks whatever happens. That is what God wants for you in Christ Jesus.*

—1 THESSALONIANS 5:16–18 NCV

I had the absolute best day today! No, it wasn't my birthday or any kind of holiday. It was just a plain old Thursday. Nothing really big happened, and to be honest, a couple of things went wrong—like missing the bus, and that reading quiz I completely forgot about. Oops! Then I got the last out in kickball after school, and my team lost.

So what made today such a great day? I *decided* it was going to be great. You see, when I woke up late this morning, I started to panic. I just *knew* it was going to be a terrible day. But then I remembered this verse I had read just last night: "Always be joyful." So I decided I would try to find something to be joyful about—no matter what went wrong. Yes, I missed the bus, but my mom handed me my favorite muffin as I rushed out the door. Then my dad drove me to school, and we sang our favorite songs as loudly as we could the whole way. No, that reading quiz wasn't my best work ever, but my teacher said I was getting better. And even though I got the last out, I had a blast hanging out with my friends.

Today was so much better than it could have been, all because I decided to look for the joy hidden in it. So here's a challenge for you: make today the absolute best day ever. Look for joy, and you'll find it.

## A BRAVE GIRL'S PRAYER

Lord, teach me to always find reasons to be joyful. Amen.

# SHARE THE GIFT

In His grace, God has given us different gifts
for doing certain things well.
—ROMANS 12:6 NLT

Faith

*Art rules*

Out of all the Brave Girls, I'm probably the quietest. I love being home with my art and my books and my Bible. And yes, I also love going out with my friends, laughing, and having fun together. But . . . it's really hard for me to reach out to people I don't know well.

So when our youth group leaders challenged us to share the good news of Jesus with others, I have to admit I was more anxious than excited. How is a quiet girl who likes to stay at home supposed to do that?

I asked my mom, and she said I should think of a way to use what I *am* good at to help me do what I'm not so good at. *Well*, I thought, *I'm good at making things. Maybe I could make something that would help me tell others about Jesus.*

That's when I had an idea! I could make beautiful paper baskets, fill them with some of Gracie's amazing Pick-Me-Up cookies, add a Bible verse, and give them to people I wanted to talk to. Because when you're sharing a gift with someone, it's much easier to share about the greatest gift of all—Jesus!

## A BRAVE GIRL'S PRAYER

Lord, teach me to use the gifts You've given me to tell others how wonderful You are. Amen.

# SHARING BASKET

This easy-to-make little basket is perfect for
sharing homemade goodies and treats!

## MATERIALS

1 large, white paper plate

pencil

tape

32-inch (82-cm) ribbon

## TOOLS

scissors

## STEPS

1. Draw four equal lines along the edge of the paper plate as shown in the picture. Then cut along those lines.

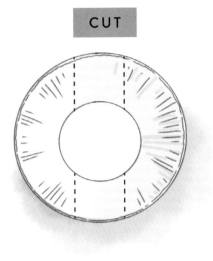

CUT

2. Fold up the four flaps.

FOLD

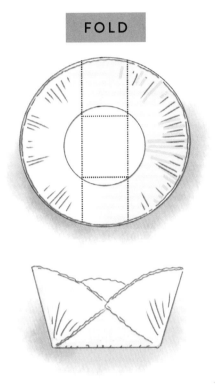

3. Hold one of the small square flaps up and fold the triangle-shaped edges of the long sides around it. Tape in place. Repeat on the other side.

4. Tie a ribbon around the basket.

Your basket is now ready to fill and give to someone special!

Glory

# ALL AROUND THE NEIGHBORHOOD

He asked Jesus, "And who is my neighbor?"
—LUKE 10:29 NLT

In Sunday school this last week, we learned about the story of the good Samaritan. You see, when Jesus was teaching on earth, He taught that we should love our neighbor as we love ourselves. But one man asked Him, "Who is my neighbor?" What the man *really* wanted was permission to say that some people were *not* his neighbor—because he didn't want to love or help everyone. That's when Jesus told the story of the Samaritan man who not only helped a total stranger but helped someone who was an enemy to the Samaritan people. Turns out, loving your neighbor means loving everyone.

I have to admit, though, that I don't even *know* all my neighbors—the ones who live right in my own neighborhood. So how could I begin to love or help them? That's when I realized that even though I didn't know how to love them, God did. And the best thing I could do was lift them up to Him in prayer. So one evening my mom and I took a walk around our neighborhood. We said hello to the neighbors we knew and introduced ourselves to those we didn't. We prayed for each person and house we passed by. And we also prayed for opportunities to show our love. Not only did I have a wonderful walk with my mom, but we met some great people.

Gather your family, take a walk around your neighborhood, and show your neighbors some love by lifting them up in prayer.

## A BRAVE GIRL'S PRAYER

Lord, I lift up my neighbors to You. Help me touch their lives with Your love. Amen.

DAY 88

*Honor*

# A LITTLE R&R

"Come to me, all of you who are tired and have heavy loads, and I will give you rest."

—MATTHEW 11:28 NCV

R&R—it stands for "rest and relaxation." And that's something we *all* need.

Even though we're young, we carry some heavy loads. And it's not just the tough days, like when we bomb a test or strike out in a game. Even all the good things, like school and church and friendships and all the other activities of everyday life, can start to just be *a lot*.

When life gets busy, or hard, or both, it's easy to forget to take care of ourselves. But the fact is that we need to take time to just be still and be with God.

When I get stressed out or when I just need a little R&R, I like to sneak away for a long soak in the tub. Maybe that sounds a little silly, but it's *sooo* relaxing. I sprinkle in some homemade bath salts (don't worry, I'll share my favorite recipe!). Then I let the water soak away all my stress. Think about it: there's no homework in the tub and no chores. It's a great place to talk to God—and don't forget to open up your heart and listen to Him too.

Do you need a little R&R today? Take a long soak in the tub. Lift your thoughts and your troubles up to God, and let Him give you rest.

## A BRAVE GIRL'S PRAYER

Lord, remind me that sometimes I need to stop and rest with You. Thank You for always being there for me. Amen.

# Soak Awhile Bath Salts

There's nothing like soaking in a hot tub after a long day of living brave. Make that soak even more relaxing with these homemade bath salts. They make wonderful gifts—for yourself or a friend.

**TIME: 20 MINUTES**

**MAKES: 3 CUPS (700 ML)**

## MATERIALS

2 cups (467 ml) Epsom salt

1/2 cup (130 g) sea salt

1/2 cup (130 g) baking soda

liquid food coloring (optional)

lavender essential oil

vanilla essential oil

3  8-ounce (250-ml) Mason jars

## TOOLS

measuring cups

mixing bowl

whisk

spoon

Experiment with different essential oils to create different scents. (Just check the labels to make sure the oil is safe for use on your skin.)

## STEPS

1. Add the Epsom salt, sea salt, and baking soda to the mixing bowl. Use the whisk to stir until thoroughly mixed.

2. Add 15 drops *total* of essential oils. If you would like more of a vanilla scent, use slightly more vanilla. If you prefer lavender, let that make up most of your drops. Stir well.

3. If you would like to color your bath salts, add five drops of liquid food coloring and stir until the color spreads evenly. (You can divide your salt mixture and use a different color for each part.)

4. Spoon into jars and seal the lids. If you have made more than one color of bath salts, layer them in the jars for a pretty effect.

5. To use, add a small scoop as you fill the bathtub.

DAY 89

# GOD'S SENSE OF HUMOR

There is a time to . . . laugh.
—ECCLESIASTES 3:4 NCV

Some people seem to think that God doesn't have a sense of humor. That it's somehow wrong—or at least, not *quite* right—to laugh and giggle and just be silly. Well, as the scientist and animal lover of the Brave Girls, I have to disagree. In fact, God is the One who invented laughter. After all, He's the One who made so many funny things. Want some proof? All it takes is a trip to the zoo (real or virtual) to prove that God loves to laugh—and to make us laugh.

I mean, how else could you possibly explain the zigzaggity, black-and-white stripes of the zebra? Or the polka dots on the long, long neck of the giraffe? (Whose tongue can be blue *or* purple, by the way!) And have you ever looked a llama in the face? That dust mop hairdo is enough to make anyone giggle!

Laughter is more than fun though; it's good for you too. A big belly laugh or a goofy giggle can make a tough day a little better. And laughter shared with a friend is the best kind of fun. The Bible even says "a cheerful heart is good medicine" (Proverbs 17:22 NIV). So if you're feeling blue, grab a friend and go check out that llama's hairdo!

## A BRAVE GIRL'S PRAYER

Lord, thank You for creating laughter. Give me plenty of reasons to giggle today! Amen.

# BE BRAVE TOGETHER

Good advice from a friend is sweet.

—PROVERBS 27:9 ICB

This whole growing-up thing isn't easy. But there are a couple of things that make it a little easier and a whole lot more fun.

The first—and most important—is to make sure you're growing up as one of God's girls. Try to follow Him in everything you do. That means filling your life with things like praise, prayer, and His Word. And it also means loving and serving others.

The second thing is having good friends who love Him too. Of course, you want to be kind and to share Jesus with everyone you can. But make sure your closest friends—the ones you're really opening up your heart to—also follow God. Trust us, it's all too easy to let fears or worries or trying to fit in pull you away from God. You need friends who will always pull you back to Him. That's what we Brave Girls try to do for each other. We hang out, giggle, encourage, and just do life together—and it's all wrapped up with a great big bow of God's love.

Create your own Brave Girls group. And don't limit your friends to people who look and talk like you. Remember, our group is all very different. There's an athlete, a fashionista, a bookworm, a singer, and an artist. Some of us are bold and busy, and others are quiet. Start with a prayer, and ask God to guide you. Then be brave and reach out to find your own Brave Girls. Because life is a whole lot better when you live it with friends—and with God!

## A BRAVE GIRL'S PRAYER

Lord, lead me to friends who not only love You but who will also love me and help me grow closer to You. Amen.